PROSLOGION II AND III

A THIRD INTERPRETATION
OF ANSELM'S ARGUMENT

PROSLOGION II AND III

A THIRD INTERPRETATION
OF ANSELM'S ARGUMENT

BY

RICHARD R. LA CROIX

LEIDEN
E. J. BRILL
1972

ISBN 90 04 03436 6

Copyright 1972 by E. J. Brill, Leiden, Netherlands

All rights reserved. No part of this book may be reproduced or translated in any form, by print, photoprint, microfilm, microfiche or any other means without written permission from the publisher

PRINTED IN THE NETHERLANDS

TABLE OF CONTENTS

PREFACE VII

ABBREVIATIONS IX

INTRODUCTION 1

I. ANSELM'S OVERALL PROGRAM IN THE *PROSLOGION* 5
 Anselm's Announced Program: the Single-Argument Claim 5
 Anselm's Actual Program 10
 The First Step of Anselm's Program 11
 The Second Step of Anselm's Program 16
 The Third or Alternative Interpretation 19
 Summary 24

II. ANSELM'S PROGRAM IN *PROSLOGION* II AND *PROSLOGION* III . . 27
 What Anselm Purports to Establish in *Proslogion* II and *Proslogion* III 27
 The *Reply* and Anselm's Single-Argument Claim 37
 The Alleged *Proslogion* III Argument 42
 The Alleged *Proslogion* II Argument 58
 A Positive Justification for the Third or Alternative Interpretation 65
 Summary 77

III. ANSELM'S REASONING 78
 The Relationship Between the *Reply* and the *Proslogion* . 78
 The Basis for the Deduction of Anselm's Existential Claims 85
 Anselm's Existential Reasoning in *Proslogion* II and III . . 101
 How *Proslogion* II and III are Taken Together 103
 The Second Sentence of the Reasoning of *Proslogion* III . 104
 The Relationship Between *Reply* I, V, and IX and Anselm's Existential Reasoning 106
 The Function of *Reply* I 107
 The First Part of *Reply* I: The Deduction of (c) 109

The Second Part of *Reply* I: The Deduction of (e) 111
The Third Part of *Reply* I: The Deduction of (d) 113
The Function of *Reply* V. 115
The Two Stages of *Reply* V: The Deduction of (d) and the
   Deduction of (c) and (e) 118
The Function of *Reply* IX 120
The Reasoning of *Reply* IX: The Deduction of (e) 121
Anselm's Single Argument. 123
An Evaluation of Anselm's Reasoning. 125

Conclusion 130

Bibliography 132

PREFACE

Because defenses and criticisms of Anselm's *Proslogion* argument for the existence of God assume that his argument has been satisfactorily identified, this book is not another defense or criticism of Anselm's argument. Instead, the purpose of this book is to identify the reasoning in and the relationship between *Proslogion* II and *Proslogion* III by arguing that there is no current philosophical interpretation of the *Proslogion* which is adequate, by offering a different philosophical interpretation which I argue is adequate, and by providing a formulation of Anselm's argument which has hitherto been unidentified. In addition, I give a brief evaluation of the newly identified argument.

Whether or not those interested in Anselm's *Proslogion* proof agree with what I represent as the third or alternative interpretation, some of them, I hope, will be convinced that uncritical representation of Anselm's argument cannot be accepted. Some, I hope, will find reasons in these pages for re-examining what commentators have in the past claimed to be Anselm's enterprise in the *Proslogion*.

I owe my appreciation to Professor D. B. Terrell of the University of Minnesota for his comments on the manuscript. A special debt of gratitude is due to Professor Gareth B. Matthews of the University of Massachusetts who was helpful in so many ways that I cannot even begin here to enumerate them.

Richard R. La Croix

ABBREVIATIONS

(a) God is that than which a greater cannot be thought.
(b) The being than-which-a-greater-cannot-be-thought exists in the mind.
(c) The being than-which-a-greater-cannot-be-thought exists in reality.
(d) The being than-which-a-greater-cannot-be-thought cannot be thought not to exist.
(e) The being than-which-a-greater-cannot-be-thought cannot not exist.
(G) God exists.
(G1) God cannot not exist.
(G2) God necessarily exists.
(G′) The being bearing the properties traditionally attributed to God exists.
(a′) The being than which a greater cannot be thought is the being bearing the properties traditionally attributed to God.
(1) If (a) and not (G), then not (c).
(2) It is not the case that both (a) and not (G).
(2′) If (a) then (G).
(1′) If (c) and (a), then (G).
(B) The being than-which-a-greater-cannot-be-thought is *not* the being than-which-a-greater-cannot-be-thought.
(f) The being than-which-a-greater-cannot-be-thought is the supreme being existing through itself alone.
(g) The being than-which-a-greater-cannot-be-thought is whatever it is better to be than not to be.
(i) a being that cannot be thought not to exist is greater than a being that can be thought not to exist.
(ia) For any x, if x cannot be thought not to exist then x is greater than what can be thought not to exist.
(ii) Something, x, can be thought to exist and cannot be thought not to exist.
(iii) x is greater than what can be thought not to exist.
(ib) Something, x, cannot be thought not to exist and x is greater than what can be thought not to exist.
(ii′) Something-than-which-a-greater-cannot-be-thought can be thought to exist and cannot be thought not to exist.
(iii′) Something-than-which-a-greater-cannot-be-thought is greater than what can be thought not to exist.
(ib′) Something-than-which-a-greater-cannot-be-thought cannot be thought not to exist and is greater than what can be thought not to exist.
(h) Existence in reality is greater than existence in the mind alone.
(G3) The being than-which-a-greater-cannot-be-thought necessarily exists.
(G4) It is necessary that the being than-which-a-greater-cannot-be-thought exists [*necesse est illud esse*].
(T) Something, x, such that nothing can be thought to be greater than x.
(T1) Something, x, such that nothing can be thought to have a degree of greatness greater than the degree of greatness which x has.
(T2) Something, x, such that nothing can be thought to have a degree of greatness greater than the degree of greatness which x has *in intellectu*.
(T3) Something, x, such that nothing can be thought to have a degree of greatness greater than the degree of greatness which x can be thought to have.
(T4) Something, x, such that nothing can be thought to be greater than x can be thought to be.

ABBREVIATIONS

(T5) Something, x, such that for *any* time t and for *any* y if x is thought at t then there is *no* time -t prior to t and there is *no* time +t subsequent to t such that x or y can at -t or +t be thought to be greater than x can be thought at t to be.

(M) It is false that something can be thought to be greater than the being than-which-a-greater-cannot-be-thought can be thought to be.

(N) Something can be thought to be greater than the being than-which-a-greater-cannot-be-thought can be thought to be.

(N1) Anything can be thought to be greater than the being than-which-a-greater-cannot-be-thought can be thought to be.

(J) The being than-which-a-greater-cannot-be-thought can be thought to be greater than the being than-which-a-greater-cannot-be-thought can be thought to be.

(J1) The being than-which-a-greater-cannot-be-thought can at t be thought to be greater than it can be thought at t' to be.

(j) The being than-which-a-greater-cannot-be-thought can be thought to be greater.

(P) If the being than-which-a-greater-cannot-be-thought can at t' be thought as it could be thought if it exists in the mind alone and the being than-which-a-greater-cannot-be-thought can at t be thought to exist in reality, then the being than-which-a-greater-cannot-be-thought can at t be thought to be greater than it can be thought at t' to be.

(l) The being than-which-a-greater-cannot-be-thought can be thought to exist in reality.

(k) The being than-which-a-greater-cannot-be-thought exists in the mind alone.

(k') The being than-which-a-greater-cannot-be-thought does not exist in reality.

(P') If the being than-which-a-greater-cannot-be-thought can at t' be thought not to exist in reality and the being than-which-a-greater-cannot-be-thought can at t be thought to exist in reality, then the being than-which-a-greater-cannot-be-thought can at t be thought to be greater than it can be thought at t' to be.

(RV) What does not exist can possibly not exist, and what can not exist can be thought of as not existing.

(S) If the being than-which-a-greater-cannot-be-thought exists in the mind alone and the being than-which-a-greater-cannot-be-thought can be thought to exist in reality, then the being than-which-a-greater-cannot-be-thought can be thought to be greater.

(P1) If the being than-which-a-greater-cannot-be-thought exists in the mind alone, then it does not exist in reality.

(P2) If the being than-which-a-greater-cannot-be-thought does not exist in reality, then it can not exist [i.e., can fail to exist] in reality.

(P3) If the being than-which-a-greater-cannot-be-thought can not exist in reality, then it can be thought not to exist in reality.

(P4) If the being than-which-a-greater-cannot-be-thought can be thought not to exist in reality and the being than-which-a-greater-cannot-be-thought can be thought to exist in reality, then the being than-which-a-greater-cannot-be-thought can be thought to be greater.

(P5) The being than-which-a-greater-cannot-be-thought can be thought to exist in reality.

(P6) It is false that the being than-which-a-greater-cannot-be-thought can be thought to be greater.

(P4') Thinking the being than-which-a-greater-cannot-be-thought to exist in reality is thinking it to be greater than thinking it not to exist in reality.

(h') Existing in reality is greater than not existing in reality.

ABBREVIATIONS

(F1)   If the being than-which-a-greater-cannot-be-thought exists in the mind alone, then it does not exist in reality.

(F2)   If the being than-which-a-greater-cannot-be-thought does not exist in reality, then it can not exist [i.e., can fail to exist] in reality.

(F3)   If the being than-which-a-greater-cannot-be-thought can not exist in reality, then it can be thought not to exist in reality.

(F4)   If the being than-which-a-greater-cannot-be-thought can be thought not to exist in reality, then it can be thought to have a beginning and an end.

(F5)   If the being than-which-a-greater-cannot-be-thought can be thought to exist in reality, then it can be thought not to have a beginning or an end.

(F6)   If the being than-which-a-greater-cannot-be-thought can be thought to have a beginning and an end and the being than-which-a-greater-cannot-be-thought can be thought not to have a beginning or an end then the being than-which-a-greater-cannot-be-thought can be thought to be greater.

(F7)   The being than-which-a-greater-cannot-be-thought can be thought to exist in reality.

(F8)   It is false that the being than-which-a-greater-cannot-be-thought can be thought to be greater.

(F6')   Thinking the being than-which-a-greater-cannot-be-thought not to have a beginning or an end is thinking it to be greater than thinking it to have a beginning and an end.

(n)   Having no beginning or end is greater than having a beginning and an end.

(o)   The being than-which-a-greater-cannot-be-thought can not exist [i.e., can fail to exist] in reality.

(m)   The being than-which-a-greater-cannot-be-thought can be thought not to exist in reality.

(p)   The being than-which-a-greater-cannot-be-thought can be thought to have a beginning and an end.

(q)   The being than-which-a-greater-cannot-be-thought can be thought not to have a beginning or an end.

(e')   The being than-which-a-greater-cannot-be-thought has neither a beginning nor an end.

(A1)   If the being than-which-a-greater-cannot-be-thought does not exist in the mind alone, then it does exist in reality.

(A2)   If the being than-which-a-greater-cannot-be-thought does exist in reality, then it can exist in reality.

(A3)   If the being than-which-a-greater-cannot-be-thought can exist in reality, then it can be thought to exist in reality.

(A4)   If the being than-which-a-greater-cannot-be-thought can be thought to exist in reality, then it can be thought not to have a beginning or an end.

(A5)   If the being than-which-a-greater-cannot-be-thought can be thought not to exist in reality, then it can be thought to have a beginning and an end.

(A6)   If the being than-which-a-greater-cannot-be-thought can be thought to have a beginning and an end and the being than-which-a-greater-cannot-be-thought can be thought not to have a beginning or an end, then the being than-which-a-greater-cannot-be-thought can be thought to be greater.

(A7)   The being than-which-a-greater-cannot-be-thought can be thought not to exist in reality.

(A8)   It is false that the being than-which-a-greater-cannot-be-thought can be thought to be greater.

(Ac)   The being than-which-a-greater-cannot-be-thought does *not* exist in reality.

(Ad)   The being than-which-a-greater-cannot-be-thought *cannot* be thought to exist.

(Ae)   The being than-which-a-greater-cannot-be-thought *cannot* exist.

(F7-1) It is possible that the being than-which-a-greater-cannot-be-thought is thought to exist in reality.
(A7-1) It is possible that the being than-which-a-greater-cannot-be-thought is thought not to exist in reality.
(F7-2) The being than-which-a-greater-cannot-be-thought is thought to exist in reality.
(A7-2) The being than-which-a-greater-cannot-be-thought is thought not to exist in reality.

INTRODUCTION

In 1078 Anselm wrote his now famous treatise, the *Proslogion*, in which he uniquely argues for the existence of God. Presumably in the same year or early in the following year, Gaunilo wrote a criticism which consists almost entirely in a critique of Chapters II and III of the *Proslogion*, and Anselm wrote a reply in which he obviously attempts to defend his reasoning in *Proslogion* II and III. Because of the importance of this discussion with Gaunilo, Anselm directed that subsequent publications of the *Proslogion* include both Gaunilo's criticism and the author's reply. From the time of Gaunilo to the Twentieth Century there has been a somewhat traditional interpretation of the *Proslogion* which has primarily two general distinctive features.

First, the traditional interpretation finds in *Proslogion* II a logically complete argument which has as its conclusion that God exists. Second, the traditional interpretation finds a complete analysis of Anselm's reasoning for the existence of God in an analysis of only *Proslogion* II. There is almost complete silence about Chapter III and Anselm's subsequent commentary in his reply to Gaunilo. The result of this silence is that almost all the discussions by commentators on Anselm's reasoning rest on this traditional interpretation and consist of defenses or criticisms of the reasoning so interpreted. For the most part, discussions of Anselm have as their main topic whether or not he committed some fallacy or mistake in *Proslogion* II. It has only been in the last few decades that commentators on Anselm have even suggested to one degree or another that there may be an alternative analysis of Anselm's reasoning for the existence of God different from the traditional interpretation;[1] and this suggestion, of course,

---

[1] The only cases that I am aware of which could be regarded as an exception to this claim occur in the works of Bonaventure and Aquinas. In *Quaestiones disputatae de mysterio Trinitatis*, question 1, article 1, Bonaventure quotes *Proslogion* III and treats it in such a way that could justifiably be interpreted as differing from the traditional interpretation and as anticipating the new interpretation, but Bonaventure's treatment does not seem to have had much influence on subsequent interpretations of the *Proslogion*. In Aquinas' *Summa Contra Gentiles*, Book 1, Chapters 10 and 11, there is an argument which employs the language of *Proslogion* III and which was undoubtedly influenced by *Proslogion* III through Bonaventure, but this argument is not represented by Aquinas as an interpretation of or commentary on Anselm. Rather, Aquinas quotes the argument in the course of what is obviously a criticism of what he

even raises the question of whether or not, or to what degree, traditional defenses and criticisms are relevant to Anselm's reasoning.

One of the more clearly defined new interpretations which preserves the obvious philosophical characteristics of Anselm's reasoning and doesn't treat it simply as a religiously spiritual discovery of God is argued for by Professor Hartshorne [2] and strongly suggested by a relatively recent and philosophically popular article by Professor Malcolm.[3] While this new interpretation of the *Proslogion* agrees with the traditional interpretation by finding in *Proslogion* II a logically complete argument the conclusion of which is that God exists, the new interpretation does not find a complete analysis of Anselm's reasoning for the existence of God in an analysis of only *Proslogion* II. The new interpretation finds in *Proslogion* III another argument which is logically independent of the argument in Chapter II and the new interpretation requires an analysis and evaluation of Chapter III in support of any claim to a complete analysis of Anselm's reasoning for the existence of God. The primary difference between the traditional interpretation and the new interpretation is that the traditional interpretation rests on the claim that there is only one argument for the existence of God in the *Proslogion* and locates it in Chapter II,[4] and the new interpretation rests on the claim that there are two logically distinct arguments for the existence of God in the *Proslogion*, one in Chapter II and one in Chapter III, such that the success or failure of one does not guarantee the success or failure of the other.

The new interpretation does little at all to challenge the traditional defenses and criticisms of Anselm's reasoning because these focus upon *Proslogion* II and so far as they go such defenses and criticisms are compatible with the new interpretation. The real challenge of the new interpretation is the suggestion that the traditional interpretation fails at least to identify fully Anselm's reasoning, and this implies that it is not a powerful enough interpretation to constitute a complete analysis or to provide grounds for a complete evaluation. In fact, the new interpretation suggests that no one in the tradition really knows what Anselm is arguing, and this is because no one in the tradition

---

takes to be Bonaventure's use of the argument to show that the existence of God is self-evident.

[2] Charles Hartshorne, *Anselm's Discovery* (La Salle, Ill.: Open Court, 1965).

[3] Norman Malcolm, "Anselm's Ontological Arguments," *Philosophical Review*, 69 (January, 1960), pp. 41-62.

[4] See footnote No. 1, above.

knows or makes clear the relationship between Chapter II and Chapter III of the *Proslogion*.

It is my intention in this discussion to examine the relationship between *Proslogion* II and III. I am not so much concerned with either developing defenses and criticisms or evaluating defenses and criticisms of Anselm's reasoning as I am concerned with the logically prior problem of discovering and stating precisely what Anselm's reasoning is in *Proslogion* II and *Proslogion* III. By examining and comparing both the new and traditional interpretations in the light of what Anselm said both in *Proslogion* II and III and in his subsequent commentary in the reply to Gaunilo, I will offer what I regard to be a plausible third or alternative interpretation of the reasoning in and the relationship between Chapters II and III of the *Proslogion*. While a commentator can never be sure that he is accurately representing the view of a philosopher, I will try to show that both the new and traditional interpretations of Anselm are inadequate to explain some of the things that Anselm both said and failed to say in the *Proslogion* and in his reply to Gaunilo, and I will argue that these inadequacies of the present interpretations suggest a plausible third or alternative interpretation.

More precisely, I will argue that the new interpretation is an inadequate interpretation of the *Proslogion* on the grounds that Chapter III does not contain a logically complete argument, and I will argue that both of the current interpretations are inadequate interpretations on the grounds that Chapter II does not contain a logically complete argument. I will try to show that *Proslogion* II and *Proslogion* III do not separately contain logically complete arguments for the existence of God, but that the two Chapters have to be taken together and that together they form the basis for a series of deductions about the existence of a being minimally characterized as that-than-which-a-greater-cannot-be-thought.[5] That is, I will try to

---

[5] Throughout this discussion I repeat Anselm's formula 'that-than-which-a-greater-cannot-be-thought' and its variation 'something-than-which-a-greater-cannot-be-thought' rather than following the practice used by most contemporary commentators of introducing an abbreviation for that formula. I do this because I regard it as an ideal in an interpretation of any philosopher to retain the original terminology as much as is possible on the grounds that significant variations on a philosopher's original terminology raise questions about the credibility of the interpretation (in this connection see the discussion, in my second chapter, of *Proslogion* III concerning the transformation of Anselm's phrase "cannot be thought not to exist"). Since Anselm himself repeats the formula instead of using an abbreviation, I also repeat the formula. The only liberty I take with Anselm's formula is to use 'the being than-which-a-

show that Anselm is attempting to establish a *series* of existential claims about that-than-which-a-greater-cannot-be-thought and that when the two Chapters are taken together a set of propositions can be identified from which this *series* of existential claims can be deduced. Finally, this third or alternative interpretation will be the basis upon which I will suggest an evaluation and criticism of Anselm's reasoning in *Proslogion* II and *Proslogion* III.

---

greater-cannot-be-thought' as a slight variation. I do this on the grounds that Anselm thinks that there is one and only one thing, actual or possible, which can be minimally characterized as that-than-which-a-greater-cannot-be-thought and that reference to 'the being so characterized' is not significantly different from reference to 'thing so characterized' or 'something so characterized.' Furthermore, I adopt Professor Charlesworth's practice of hyphenating the formula. This is not meant to imply that the formula designates a simple predicate as opposed to a complex predicate. The practice of hyphenating the formula is only a convention intended for convenience in reading in lieu of an abbreviation.

CHAPTER ONE

ANSELM'S OVERALL PROGRAM IN THE *PROSLOGION*

The primary concern of this discussion is the reasoning in and the relationship between *Proslogion* II and III. However, it is extremely important to realize that the third or alternative interpretation is suggested not only by the proposed internal analysis of *Proslogion* II and III and Anselm's subsequent commentary on these Chapters in his reply to Gaunilo, but it is also suggested by an external examination and analysis of Anselm's overall program and procedure in the *Proslogion* as a whole, both as that program is announced in the *Preface* and as it is in fact carried out. So, before beginning a detailed analysis of the relationship between *Proslogion* II and III, it is perhaps advisable at the outset to make some remarks about the relationship of these two Chapters to the *Proslogion* as a whole and to make a clear distinction between those Anselmian claims which fall within the scope of Chapters II and III and those Anselmian claims which fall within the scope of the *Proslogion* but outside the scope of Chapters II and III.

Anselm's Announced Program: The Single-Argument Claim

In his *Preface* to the *Proslogion* Anselm announces his intended program by comparing it with the program he followed in the *Monologion*.

> After I had published, at the pressing entreaties of several of my brethren, a certain short tract [the *Monologion*] as an example of meditation on the meaning of faith from the point of view of one seeking, through silent reasoning within himself, things he knows not—reflecting that this was made up of a connected chain of many arguments, I began to wonder if perhaps it might be possible to find *one single argument* that for its proof required no other save itself, and that by itself would suffice to prove that *God really exists*, that *He is the supreme good needing no other* and is He whom all things have need of for their being and well-being, and also *to prove whatever we believe about the Divine Being*.[1] (Italics mine.)

---

[1] Anselm, *St. Anselm's Proslogion with a Reply on Behalf of the Fool by Gaunilo and the Author's Reply to Gaunilo*, trans. with an introduction and philosophical commentary by M.J. Charlesworth (Oxford: Clarendon Press, 1965), p. 103.

Of course Anselm thought that he had found such an argument and regarded it as being represented in the *Proslogion*. The most significant feature of this announced program for the *Proslogion* is that it is to contain *one single argument* as contrasted with the connected chain of *many arguments* of the *Monologion*. Accordingly, if Anselm's actual program corresponds to his announced program, the problem is to locate this one single argument.

It is difficult to know how the current interpretations would deal with Anselm's single-argument claim, since almost none of the commentators even mention the *Preface* or the claim. Nevertheless, it seems that if we follow the traditional interpretation, then presumably the single argument is to be located in *Proslogion* II, since the traditional interpretation finds there both a logically complete argument whose conclusion is that God exists and, at least implicitly, a complete analysis of Anselm's reasoning. It is not possible to give such an easy account of how the proponents of the new interpretation would deal with Anselm's single-argument claim, because while they agree with the traditional* interpretation in locating in Chapter II a logically complete argument whose conclusion is that God exists, they also locate in Chapter III an additional and different logically complete argument. Furthermore, while all of these proponents find the reasoning in Chapter II to be invalid, some of them like Malcolm and Hartshorne, find the reasoning in Chapter III to be valid and others like Professor Charlesworth find the reasoning in Chapter III to be invalid but, nevertheless, independent of Chapter II.

In any case, the new interpretation in fact finds two arguments in the *Proslogion* and, hence, could not "locate" a single argument. In view of this fact, the only way that the new interpretation could deal with Anselm's single-argument claim would be to deny that Anselm's actual program corresponds to his announced program. This is the approach that is taken by Charlesworth in his commentary on the *Proslogion*, the only commentary I am aware of that includes an analysis of the *Preface* and specifically mentions the single-argument claim.[2] Charlesworth explains that in the light of the single-argument claim Anselm probably regarded the argument in Chapter III as a

---

[2] Karl Barth mentions the single-argument claim in the Introduction of his book on Anselm but immediately identifies it with Anselm's formula for God and then dismisses it. (*Anselm: Fides Quaerens Intellectum* [John Knox Press: Richmond, Virginia, 1960], pp. 13-14.)

complement to the basic argument in Chapter II, but he concludes that despite Anselm's intentions the Chapter III proof is logically independent of the proof in Chapter II.[3] In other words, presumably Anselm's actual program does not correspond to his announced program.

While Malcolm doesn't specifically mention the single-argument claim, he does say that in the *Proslogion* there are two different pieces of reasoning which Anselm did not distinguish from one another and that there is no evidence that Anselm thought of himself as offering two different proofs. This might be interpreted as an offhand reference or acknowledgment of Anselm's single-argument claim. Despite this, however, Malcolm proceeds to tell us what Anselm says in *Proslogion* II and III and concludes that there are in fact two different proofs.[4] In other words, presumably Anselm's actual program fails to correspond to his announced program.

The initial problem of locating Anselm's single argument is thus solved in the traditional view by locating it in *Proslogion* II, and in the new view the problem is solved by claiming that there is not just one single argument but rather two logically independent arguments. Unfortunately, neither of these solutions taken separately is an adequate solution nor taken together do they exhaust the possibilities of solution. Not one proponent of the new interpretation ever bothers to show or argue that *Proslogion* III contains a logically complete argument. Instead, they begin by assuming with the traditional interpretation that Chapter II contains a logically complete argument, though an invalid one, and then point out that Chapter III contains the formula "cannot be thought not to exist" which is not contained in Chapter II. On the basis of this formula, they contruct an argument and then claim that Chapter III contains that argument. Not one of the proponents of this view tries to show that Anselm is in fact reasoning according to the constructed argument. It is one thing to show that an argument can be *constructed* around some comments or claims made by a philosopher and still another thing to show that those comments and claims as they are made and related to one another actually constitute an argument by that philosopher. I know of no commentator who tries to show by textual analysis or any

---

[3] Anselm, pp. 73-74.
[4] Norman Malcolm, "Anselm's Ontological Arguments," *Philosophical Review*, 69 (January, 1960), pp. 45-51.

other way that the argument he constructs from *Proslogion* III is actually contained in that Chapter.

The general problem before us is to discover exactly what Anselm's reasoning is in *Proslogion* II and III, and the immediate problem is to locate his alleged single argument. To discover what argument can be constructed from remarks made by Anselm does not further our purpose unless we can also discover that the constructed arguments are also actual Anselmian arguments or at least discover that Chapter III does contain some argument or other. Not only do the proponents of the new interpretation fail to show that their constructed arguments are actual Anselmian arguments, they also fail to show that Chapter III contains any argument at all.

I will argue in my next chapter that Anselm's comments and claims as they are made and related to one another in the first paragraph of *Proslogion* III can be interpreted as constituting an argument only if we are willing to attribute unto Anselm a very trivial argument, and, even then, that argument doesn't correspond to the constructed arguments of the new interpretation. Despite this fact, however, it would hardly be an adequate solution to the problem of locating Anselm's single argument to say that there is no single argument but rather two arguments and that Anselm's actual program fails to correspond to his announced program unless it were soundly established either that the constructed arguments are also actual Anselmian arguments or at least that there is some logically complete argument or other in *Proslogion* III. The result, then, is that the new interpretation with its claim to locate two arguments in the *Proslogion*, one in Chapter II and one in Chapter III, is incompatible with Anselm's single-argument claim and is, at least without further work, incapable of explaining away the claim except by fiat. This fact surely suggests the possibility of an alternative interpretation, for in the absence of evidence to the contrary, it might turn out that there is an adequate interpretation of the *Proslogion* in which Anselm does present one single argument which can be located.

One possibility that immediately suggests itself is to follow the traditional interpretation and locate the single argument in Chapter II while reserving the right to bolster that argument with claims made in Chapter III. But this approach assumes that the traditional interpretation can provide an adequate solution to the problem by locating Anselm's single argument in Chapter II. This is not the case. In fact, any interpretation that attempts to locate Anselm's single argument in any one chapter is doomed to failure because there is no single chapter, nor any two that can be taken together for that matter, from which an argument can be constructed or in which an argument can be found that conforms to the characteristics Anselm attributes to his single argument. For, in the *Preface*, Anselm claims not only to have discovered one single argument as contrasted with a connected chain of many arguments but to have discovered one single argument that for its proof requires no other save itself, and that by itself would suffice to prove not only that God really exists but that He is the supreme good needing no other, and also to prove *whatever* we believe about the Divine Being. Surely even a cursory reading of Chapters II and III makes it plain that Anselm could not have intended these Chapters either singly or taken together to represent his one single argument. Even taken together, the scope of these two Chapters hardly encompasses *whatever* is believed about the Divine Being. The broadest possible scope that can be claimed for these two Chapters is that they encompass a certain set of existential claims.

It turns out that Anselm's single argument can be identified neither with Chapter II or Chapter III nor can it be identified with the two Chapters taken together, so that neither of the current interpretations can provide an adequate solution to the problem of locating Anselm's single argument nor do they provide reason for assuming that Anselm's announced program fails to correspond to his actual program. Again, it requires only a cursory reading of the entire *Proslogion* to see that it is the *Proslogion* as a whole which corresponds to Anselm's intention of providing one single argument that for its proof requires no other save itself, and that by itself would suffice to prove that God really exists, that He is the supreme good needing no other and is He whom all things have need of for their being and well-being, and also to prove whatever we believe about the Divine Being.

If this is indeed Anselm's program in the *Proslogion*, then it surely suggests both the possibility of interpreting Chapters II and III not as discrete arguments for the existence of God but, rather, as a series of deductions about the existence of a being minimally characterized as that-than-which-a-greater-cannot-be-thought and the possibility of interpreting the remainder of the *Proslogion* as a series of deductions about the further nature of this being where both series of deductions taken as a whole constitute Anselm's one single argument. Anselm's argument, then, could be regarded as one single argument with two stages. The first stage would be the existential deductions of *Proslogion* II and III, and the second stage would be the theistic deductions of the remainder of the *Proslogion* where all the deductions are taken to be deductions about that-than-which-a-greater-cannot-be-thought. The first stage would show that the being exists and the second stage would show that the being is God.

Anselm's Actual Program

When we turn to a closer examination of Anselm's actual program, the same possibilities of interpretation are suggested even without appealing, as a directive for interpretation, to his program as it is announced in the *Preface*; for it turns out that it is the entire *Proslogion* which is intended to establish the existence of God; that is, it is the entire *Proslogion* which is intended to establish both that a being exists and to establish that the being whose existence is established does bear the properties traditionally attributed to God. In order to establish the existence of God on Anselm's view, it is not sufficient to show that a being characterized in some unique way exists and then simply stipulate that the uniquely characterized being is God or simply stipulate that the being bears the properties traditionally attributed to God. On Anselm's view in the *Proslogion*, to establish the existence of God it is necessary to show not only that a uniquely characterized being exists, but it is also necessary to show that the uniquely characterized being *does* bear the properties traditionally attributed to God. In other words, it is necessary to establish both existence and Godhood.

Corresponding to these requirements, Anselm's actual program in the *Proslogion* is to characterize God in a certain minimal way and then to establish first that a being so characterized exists and, second, to establish that the being so characterized bears the properties traditionally attributed to God. More precisely, Anselm's actual program in the *Proslogion* is to characterize God minimally as that-than-which-a-greater-cannot-be-thought and then to establish first the existence and something about the existence of the being than-which-a-greater-cannot-be-thought and, second, to establish that the being than-which-a-greater-cannot-be-thought also bears the properties traditionally attributed to God. The two claims, that the being than-which-a-greater-cannot-be-thought exists and that the being than-which-a-greater-cannot-be-thought bears the properties traditionally attributed to God, when taken together constitute the claim that God exists, and, hence, the two steps of Anselm's program when taken together constitute Anselm's proof for the existence of God.

The First Step of Anselm's Program

The first step of Anselm's program is the task of *Proslogion* II and III and is reiterated and expanded in the *Reply*. The problem of interpretation at this point is to describe as accurately as possible what the strongest claims are that Anselm purports or could possibly purport to establish in the reasoning of *Proslogion* II and III and to provide some textual justification for supposing that Anselm purports to establish these claims. On most interpretations it is held that either one or both of these Chapters contain a logically complete argument, and it is held that the argument is intended by Anselm to establish the claim that God exists. I believe that both of these suppositions are wrong. I think that it is a mistake to suppose that Anselm purports to establish the claim that God exists in either of these two Chapters alone and I think that it is a mistake to treat either one or both of these Chapters as discrete arguments and especially, of course, as discrete arguments to establish the claim that God exists.

Both mistakes, it seems to me, rest on the failure to understand both the relationship that obtains between *Proslogion* II and *Proslogion* III and the relationship that obtains between these two Chapters and the remainder of the *Proslogion*. The first assumption that Anselm purports to establish the claim that God exists can be seen to be a mistake when we examine the actual claims that Anselm makes in *Proslogion* II and III. The second assumption that *Proslogion* II, or *Proslogion* II and III, represent discrete arguments independent and complete in themselves can be seen to be at least questionable once we have seen what claims Anselm makes in the *Proslogion*, what claims Anselm purports to establish in *Proslogion* II and III, the relationship that is intended to obtain between these two sets of claims, and from what basic assumptions these claims are supposed to follow.

When we examine *Proslogion* II and III and list in order the assertions made by Anselm that could possibly count as claims which

Anselm is attempting to establish, we find that he asserts the following propositions:

(a) God is that than which a greater cannot be thought. (*Proslogion* II)
(b) The being than-which-a-greater-cannot-be-thought exists in the mind. (*Proslogion* II)
(c) The being than-which-a-greater-cannot-be-thought exists in reality. (*Proslogion* II and III)
(d) The being than-which-a-greater-cannot-be-thought cannot be thought not to exist. (*Proslogion* III)
(e) The being than-which-a-greater-cannot-be-thought cannot not exist.[5] (*Proslogion* III)

The first significant thing to notice is that nowhere in *Proslogion* II or III does Anselm assert explicitly that God exists, but on most interpretations it is held that Anselm purports to establish there the claim that God exists. It is hard to see how Anselm can be regarded as purporting to establish a claim he doesn't even make there. However, there are two ways by which a justification might be made for interpreting *Proslogion* II or *Proslogion* III as containing, at least implicitly, the claim

(G) God exists.

The first way is to take assertions (a) and (c) as constituting, for Anselm, the claim (G). It could then be argued that (G) is the implicit claim made by Anselm when his explicit claims (a) and (c) are taken together. The second way is to take assertions (a) and (e) as constituting, for Anselm, the claim (G). According to this approach it could be argued that (G) is the implicit claim made by Anselm when his explicit claims (a) and (e) are taken together.[6] In fact it might be

---

[5] I list (d) and (e) separately. Commentators such as Hartshorne, Malcolm, and Charlesworth treat (e) as the meaning of (d) where "cannot not exist" is equivalent to "necessarily exists." In my next chapter I shall argue that "cannot not exist" is not, for Anselm, equivalent to "necessarily exists," where this latter phrase is usually meant to denote logical necessity. Furthermore, I shall argue that (d) and (e) are, for Anselm, separate and distinct claims, but the arguments of my present chapter do not depend on whether or not (d) and (e) are separate and distinct claims. Consequently, listing (d) and (e) separately could, at this point, result only in the charge that I have been redundant in listing Anselm's claims.

[6] To be quite accurate we would have to say that (a) and (e) taken together imply
  (G1) God cannot not exist

argued that in the last paragraph of *Proslogion* III Anselm is both actually arguing in this latter way and explicitly asserting (G). In this passage Anselm says:

> And You, Lord our God, are this being. You exist so truly, Lord my God, that You cannot even be thought not to exist.[7]

Consequently it might be supposed that since the first sentence is equivalent to assertion (a), then what Anselm asserts in the second sentence is (G) where the second sentence is intended implicitly to follow from (a) and (d) or from (a) and (e). However, it is highly doubtful that Anselm intended this passage either to be an argument or to express any factual assertions about God. The nature of this passage suggests that it is simply intended to be a digressive address to God concerning certain of Anselm's *beliefs* about the nature of God. The position of this passage further suggests that it is an assertion of these beliefs on the basis of a privileged insight that what holds true of the being than-which-a-greater-cannot-be-thought holds true of God as well; an insight, which I shall try to show later, that Anselm subsequently attempts to explicate and substantiate. As such, this passage does not contain any statements which make a factual assertion about the nature of God, but, rather, it contains statements which make assertions about Anselm's beliefs about the nature of God. More precisely, the major claim or assertion contained in this passage is "I believe God exists" and not the assertion or claim "God exists."

Nevertheless, even if we grant that (a) and (c) taken together or (a) and (e) taken together implies (G) and, hence, that (G) is contained implicitly in *Proslogion* II or III or even if we grant that (G) occurs explicitly there, it does not follow that Anselm purports to *establish* (G) in the last paragraph of *Proslogion* III or anywhere else in these two Chapters. While it is true that Anselm attempts to establish (b), (c), (d), and (e) in these two Chapters, he only asserts (a) and does not try to establish it, so that while *asserted* (a) taken together with *established* (c) or *established* (e) might be taken as implying (G), it can't be taken as establishing (G) or even as an attempt at establishing

---

where for the proponents of the new interpretation (G1) would mean

(G2) God necessarily exists.

But since (G1) and (G2) are thought to imply (G), if (a) and (e) taken together imply (G1) and (G2) then (a) and (e) taken together imply (G) for the proponents of the new interpretation.

[7] Anselm, p. 119.

(G). The fact that Anselm asserts (a) is no more justification on the part of commentators for assuming that Anselm purports to establish (G) from the fact that he purports to establish (c) and (e) than it would be a justification on the part of Anselm for claiming that he has established (G) by having established (c) and (e). Of course, Anselm does not in *Proslogion* II or III claim to have established (G).

However, it might be argued in rebuttal that Anselm did not try to establish (a) because assertion (a) functions in Anselm's procedure as a definition of "God", and definitions are not required to be established.[8] Consequently, while the definition is a weak link in Anselm's argument insofar as there is no obligation to accept it, the attempt to establish (c) and (e) taken together with the definition (a) constitutes Anselm's attempt to establish (G). The problem with this rebuttal is that Anselm gives no indication in either *Proslogion* II or *Proslogion* III that (a) is to be taken as a definition of "God", and some justification must be given for interpreting (a) as a definition other than the fact that such an interpretation allows us to prove that Anselm purports to establish (G) in *Proslogion* II and III alone. There is no dispute that (a) can be taken as a definition of "God", but that it can be so interpreted does not show that this was Anselm's intention.

It must be kept in mind that the task here is to discover what Anselm's reasoning is in *Proslogion* II and III and not to discover what reasoning can be constructed out of the assertions that Anselm makes. The fact that we can prove the desired conclusion from the interpretation does not establish that this is in fact Anselm's procedure. The question before us now is whether or not Anselm purports to establish (G) in *Proslogion* II and III; and from the fact that there is an interpretation of (a) which implies that Anselm does purport to establish (G) there, it does not follow that the interpretation corresponds to Anselm's procedure. The truth is that there is no justification in *Proslogion* II or III for commentators to treat (a) as a definition of "God" unless these Chapters are approached with the preconceived notion that Anselm is attempting to establish (G) in these passages alone, and whether or not Anselm is attempting to establish (G) in these passages alone should be the result of analysis, not the directive for analysis.

Furthermore, aside from the fact that Anselm gives no indication that (a) is intended as a definition of "God", treating (a) as a definition

---

[8] All commentators that I am aware of either explicitly state that (a) is a definition or else treat it as a definition.

has results that make the assumption highly questionable. While it is true that (G) is implied by (a) and (c) taken together as well as (a) and (e) taken together and that (a) and (G) taken together imply (c), the assumption that (a) functions in Anselm's procedure as a definition of "God" has the result that (G) *means* (c) for Anselm.[9] This result casts a great deal of doubt on the adequacy of any approach that interprets *Proslogion* II or III as Anselm's attempt to establish claim (G) on the grounds that (a) is a definition of "God" because it is highly doubtful that (G) means (c) for Anselm; and if it does not, then (a) does not function as a definition of "God" in his procedure and *Proslogion* II and III alone do not represent Anselm's attempt at establishing (G).

The assumption that (a) functions in Anselm's procedure as a definition of "God" is presumably the result of recognizing the fact that while the reasoning of *Proslogion* II and III is clearly philosophical, Anselm also intended it to have some religious significance which (c) alone surely does not have, so that by taking (a) as a definition of "God" and conjoining it with (c), the conjunction presumably implies the religiously significant claim (G). The merit of this approach is that it recognizes that Anselm clearly intended *Proslogion* II and III to have some religious significance and that for Anselm (G) *must* be religiously significant wherever it occurs. What is not noticed in this approach is that treating (a) as a definition of "God" does not confer religious significance upon (c), rather in the process of treating (a) as a definition of "God", (G) is stripped of its usual religious significance by being made equivalent in meaning to (c). The result is that if the meaning of (G) is to have some religious significance for Anselm which (c) alone does not have, then (G) does not mean (c) and, hence, (a) does not function in Anselm's procedure as a definition of "God". That this is the case should be obvious from the fact that if (G) is to have any religious significance for Anselm, then (G) must be equivalent in meaning not to (c), but to something like:

(G′) The being bearing the properties traditionally attributed to God exists

---

[9] Similarly if (a) is a definition of "God" then (G1), namely, God cannot not exist, *means* (e) for Anselm. Consequently, in what follows I will mention only (c) and the relation of (c) to (a) and (G) because what holds true of (c) holds true *mutatis mutandis* of (e) and what holds true of the relation of (c) to (a) and (G) holds true *mutatis mutandis* of the relation of (e) to (a) and (G1) and since (G1) is thought to imply (G), to (G) as well.

and surely neither (a) and (c) nor (a) and (e) implies (G') if (a) is treated as a definition of "God". Consequently, if (G) means (G') for Anselm then (a) does not function as a definition of "God" in Anselm's procedure and it cannot be claimed that Anselm had no need to establish (a) as well as (c) and (e) in order to establish (G).

In order to establish or purport to establish claim (G) in *Proslogion* II and III alone, Anselm would be required to establish, or at least attempt to establish, not only (c) and (e); he would also have to attempt to establish, not just assert, claim (a). It might, for example, be the case that the being than-which-a-greater-cannot-be-thought exists and turn out that, after all, the being is, alas, not God. What would count as establishing (a) would be to establish some proposition like:

> (a') The being than which a greater cannot be thought is the being bearing the properties traditionally attributed to God.

If Anselm had established or attempted to establish (a') or something like (a') in *Proslogion* II or *Proslogion* III, then the claim that Anselm purports to establish (G) in *Proslogion* II alone or *Proslogion* II and III alone could be substantiated by pointing out that (a') and (c) or (a') and (e) surely do imply (G') and, hence, (G). Furthermore, it could then be argued that since Anselm purports to establish (c), (e), and (a'), he at least implicitly purports to establish (G) in *Proslogion* II and III. Unfortunately for the current interpretations Anselm does not purport to establish (a') in either *Proslogion* II or III. The strongest possible claims that Anselm could purport to *establish* in *Proslogion* II and III are that the being than-which-a-greater-cannot-be-thought exists; that the being than-which-a-greater-cannot-be-thought cannot be thought not to exist; and, as I shall try to show in my next chapter, that the being than-which-a-greater-cannot-be-thought cannot not exist; that is, (c), (d), and (e).

The Second Step of Anselm's Program

However, there is a very good reason why Anselm does not attempt to establish (a') in *Proslogion* II or III, and it provides an additional reason why (a) or (a') does not function in Anselm's procedure as a definition of "God". The reason is that Anselm employed *Proslogion* II and III to fulfill the task of establishing (b), (c), (d), and (e) while the chapters subsequent to *Proslogion* IV are intended to establish something like (a'). This is in fact Anselm's second step of the proof which begins with *Proslogion* V in which Anselm attempts to do two things concurrently. He attempts to show that the being than-which-a-greater-cannot-be-thought is the supreme being existing through itself alone; and that the being is perceptive, omnipotent, merciful, and impassible; and that the being is whatever is believed about the Divine Being. In other words, Anselm attempts to *establish* a series of claims about the being than-which-a-greater-cannot-be-thought such that the series of claims implies (a'). In short, Anselm attempts to establish (a') in the chapters subsequent to *Proslogion* IV such that (c) and (a') imply (G') and, hence (G) and such that it is the entire *Proslogion* which is intended to establish (G). Concurrently Anselm also attempts an apologetic to show how these theistic properties can be consistently attributed to the being than-which-a-greater-cannot-be-thought.

Anselm's procedure, to oversimplify, is to first establish the existence and something about the existence of a being and, second, to establish that the being is God. This task requires the entire *Proslogion*. However, if we ignore or disregard the second step of Anselm's proof in the chapters subsequent to *Proslogion* IV, then from the fact that he attempts to establish, among other things, that a being exists which is characterized as that-than-which-a-greater-cannot-be-thought and *asserts* in *Proslogion* II, III, and IV that God is this being, then it is natural enough to interpret *Proslogion* II or III as an attempt to establish the existence of God in the absence of any other way of accounting for Anselm's reason for establishing (c) in the context of asserting (a). Despite the naturalness of this interpretation, Anselm makes it quite clear in the beginning of *Proslogion* II that the immediate problem to which he is going to address himself is the status of the being characterized as that-than-which-a-greater-cannot-be-thought. He says

> Now we believe that You are something than which nothing greater can be thought. Or can it be that a thing of such a nature does not exist, since 'the Fool has said in his heart, there is no God' [Ps. xiii. I, lii. I]? [10]

The question that Anselm poses is not whether (G) is true or false, but whether (c) is true or false, and the remainder of *Proslogion* II

---

[10] Anselm, p. 117.

and half of *Proslogion* III is devoted to establishing the existence and the nature of the existence of this being. The point of these two Chapters is to show the Fool that he can't consistently deny the existence of the being than-which-a-greater-cannot-be-thought. To be sure, the problem of whether (c) is true or false arises *in part* from the fact that the Fool denies that (G) is true, but Anselm's aim in *Proslogion* II and III is to show that while the Fool denies the truth of (G), he cannot consistently deny the truth of (c). The ultimate point, of course, is to be that if the Fool cannot consistently deny the truth of (c), then he cannot consistently deny the truth of (G) either, but the falsity of (c) is not implied by the falsity of (G) alone. The falsity of (c) is implied by the truth of (a) and the falsity of (G). What Anselm is saying in the above quotation is

(1) If (a) and not (G), then not (c)

so that if it can be established that (c) cannot be consistently denied, that is that (c) is true, then it follows that

(2) It is not the case that both (a) and not (G)

and (2) is equivalent to

(2′) If (a) then (G).

Even when we take assertions (d) and (e) which are established in *Proslogion* II and III as a partial determination of the theistic attributes, that determination would not be broad enough to claim that Anselm had established or attempted to establish assertion (a). The strongest claim that the combined reasoning of *Proslogion* II and III can possibly establish is not (G) but (2′), and since (1) is equivalent to

(1′) If (c) and (a), then (G),

it is reasonable enough to interpret (1) as a statement of Anselm's program which is carried out by establishing (c) in *Proslogion* II and III and establishing (a) in the chapters subsequent to *Proslogion* IV so that (G) follows from (c) and (a).

Proslogion II and III do not *establish* nor are they intended to *establish* (G) by themselves. The only force these Chapters have by themselves is to enable one to *understand* that (G) is true providing he *understands* that (a) is true and that he understands the proof that establishes (c). While *Proslogion* II and *Proslogion* III are clearly intended to establish that (c) cannot be consistently denied, in *Proslogion* IV Anselm makes it quite plain that there are conditions under which (G) *can* be consistently denied and conditions under which (G) *cannot* be consistently denied. In Chapter IV Anselm says

> In the first sense, then, God can be thought not to exist, but not at all in the second sense. No one, indeed, understanding what God is can think that God does not exist, even though he may say these words in his heart either without any [objective] signification or with some peculiar signification. For God is that-than-which-nothing-greater-can-be-thought.[11]

Under the condition that God is not understood or thought to be the being mentioned in (c), that is, if God's nature is not understood or thought to be described by (a), then (G) can be consistently denied. On the other hand (G) cannot be consistently denied only if (a) is understood to describe God's nature. Consequently, *Proslogion* II and III do not establish (G) unless understanding that (a) is true consists in understanding a proof that establishes (a). If understanding that (a) is true consists in simply believing that (a) is true or assuming that (a) is true, then understanding that (a) is true commits one to believing or accepting (G) on the basis of understanding the proof for (c). However, such an understanding of (a) does not count as establishing (G), and while Anselm believes (a) independently he certainly sees the need for establishing it and begins to do so in the very next Chapter.

The net result is that *Proslogion* II and III do not represent Anselm's attempt at establishing (G). Rather, it is the entire *Proslogion* that is intended to establish (G). Anselm's actual procedure is to establish (b), (c), (d), and (e) in *Proslogion* II and III, and in the chapters subsequent to *Proslogion* IV to establish a series of propositions which in conjunction with (d) and (e) imply (a′) such that (c) and (a′) taken together imply (G). Consequently neither *Proslogion* II nor *Proslogion* II and III are adequately interpreted as Anselm's attempt at establishing the claim that God exists.

The Third Or Alternative Interpretation

So far I have tried to show that when we examine Anselm's actual procedure in the *Proslogion*, both the traditional interpretation and

---

[11] Anselm, p. 121.

the new interpretation are inadequate interpretations of Anselm's reasoning. The traditional interpretation which treats *Proslogion* II as a discrete and independent argument whose conclusion is (G) is inadequate on the grounds that *Proslogion* II alone does not represent Anselm's attempt at establishing the claim (G). The new interpretation which treats *Proslogion* II as one discrete and independent argument whose conclusion is (G) and which treats *Proslogion* III as an additional discrete and independent argument whose conclusion is (G) is inadequate on the grounds that neither *Proslogion* II alone nor *Proslogion* III alone nor the two Chapters taken together represent Anselm's attempt at establishing the claim (G). The failure of these interpretations to recognize the fact that neither of these two Chapters is intended to establish (G) rests on the failure to understand the relationship that obtains between the several chapters of the *Proslogion*.

A further result of failing to understand this relationship is that both interpretations are also inadequate because they treat either *Proslogion* II or *Proslogion* II and III as discrete and independent arguments. If *Proslogion* II and III are not intended to establish the claim that God exists, then it follows, of course, that *Proslogion* II and III do not represent *arguments* intended to establish the claim that God exists. Nevertheless the question remains whether or not *Proslogion* II or *Proslogion* II and III can be adequately interpreted as discrete and independent arguments for any claim at all. Simply because the proponents of the current interpretations are wrong in thinking that Anselm was attempting to establish (G) in these two Chapters, it does not follow that they are wrong in thinking that these two Chapters represent discrete and independent arguments, nor does it follow that their formulations of the arguments are entirely wrong.

It might be argued that the analyses by the proponents of the current interpretations are correct insofar as they formulate Anselm's argument in *Proslogion* II and wrong only in their interpretation of Anselm's logical move between (a) and (c), because the basic reasoning of *Proslogion* II is intended to establish (c) and the basic analyses by the proponents of both the traditional and new interpretations of the reasoning of *Proslogion* II is consistent with treating (c) rather than (G) as the conclusion of the argument they identify. Similarly, it might be argued that the analysis by the proponents of the new interpretation is correct insofar as it formulates Anselm's argument in *Proslogion* III and wrong only in its interpretation of Anselm's logical move between (a) and (e), because the basic reasoning of *Proslogion* III is intended to establish (e) and the basic analysis by the proponents of the new interpretation of the reasoning of *Proslogion* III is consistent with treating (e) rather than (G) as the conclusion of the argument it identifies.

But while it is true that the primary task of *Proslogion* II is to establish the claim (c) and the primary task of *Proslogion* III is to establish the claim (e), it does not follow from this that *Proslogion* II and *Proslogion* III are intended to be discrete and independent arguments such that one argument is intended to establish (c) and the other argument is intended to establish (e). The simple fact that the analyses of the reasoning in *Proslogion* II and III given by the current interpretations is consistent with treating (c) and (e) as conclusions of these two Chapters respectively, when they are treated as discrete and independent arguments, does not imply that the treatments or the formulations correspond to Anselm's procedure. That a philosopher reasons or attempts to establish some claim does, of course, imply that there is an argument, but the fact that a philosopher reasons in two or more successive chapters even when there are two or more successive claims involved does not imply that there are two or more successive arguments. It may be that the reasoning and, hence, the argument spans the two or more successive chapters where the successive claims involved represent steps in a series of deductions from one set of premises. Whether a philosopher's reasoning represents one complex argument or one simple argument or a series of arguments is a question whose answer needs to be established and not simply assumed if a treatment of that philosopher's view purports to be an adequate interpretation of that view.

With respect to the *Proslogion*, the number of arguments or how they are to be counted and identified is never established nor, for that matter, even discussed; it is always assumed. Consequently, in the face of my objection that neither *Proslogion* II alone nor *Proslogion* III alone can be adequately interpreted as Anselm's attempt at establishing (G), proponents of the current interpretations cannot adequately modify their views simply by changing their claims concerning what conclusion Anselm intended to establish and still maintain that these two Chapters represent discrete and independent arguments unless some textual justification is given for treating them as independent arguments. Textual justification for such a position would, I believe, be difficult to find if the relationship between *Proslogion* II and *Proslogion* III and the relationship of these two Chapters to the remainder of the *Proslogion* is carefully considered. If these relationships are ignored, then, like the assumption that Anselm intended to establish claim (G) in *Proslogion* II and *Proslogion* III, the assumption that *Proslogion* II or *Proslogion* II and III represent complete and independent arguments is the only reasonable principle to guide an interpretation. What is not reasonable or justifiable is to disregard the relationships that exist between the various chapters, and what is not adequate is an interpretation that does disregard these relationships.

So far I have argued only that treating *Proslogion* II or *Proslogion* II and III as complete and independent arguments has never been justified by any commentator and that Anselm's procedure doesn't imply that these Chapters ought to be so treated. I have also tried to show that treating these Chapters as complete and independent arguments is at least questionable because they are treated as arguments intended to establish (G) and Anselm does not purport to establish (G) in these Chapters. However, showing these things does not definitively establish that these Chapters are not intended to be complete and independent arguments nor that such a view cannot be justified. Nevertheless, it must be kept in mind that the present task is to show that an external examination of Anselm's actual procedure in the *Proslogion* suggests a third and plausible alternative interpretation of *Proslogion* II and III in the same way that Anselm's announced procedure of the *Preface* suggests such an alternative interpretation. Surely the facts that Anselm intends to establish (G) in the *Proslogion* as a whole, that he does not purport to establish (G) in either *Proslogion* II alone or *Proslogion* III alone, and that the claims of *Proslogion* II and III and of the chapters subsequent to *Proslogion* IV when taken together imply (G) suggest the possibility of treating the entire *Proslogion* as one single argument. And, indeed, it also suggests the possibility of treating the claims and reasoning of *Proslogion* II and III as well as the claims and reasoning of the chapters subsequent to *Proslogion* IV as the process of making deductions from one central set of premises.

What further suggests the possibility of such an interpretation is the fact that the claims of the various chapters are all claims about the being than-which-a-greater-cannot-be-thought and in each case what Anselm is trying to establish is that the truth of some proposition about this being is deducible from the fact that the being is that-than-which-a-greater-cannot-be-thought.

The feature that distinguishes what we have been calling the two steps of Anselm's proof is not that they represent two discrete arguments or two different types of reasoning, but rather that they represent two different types of claims about this being which are deducible from the fact that the being is that-than-which-a-greater-cannot-be-thought. What distinguishes the first step consisting of *Proslogion* II and III from the second step consisting of the chapters subsequent to *Proslogion* IV is that the first step represents deductions about the existence of this being and the second step represents deductions about the theistic attributes of this being. Similarly, what distinguishes the reasoning of *Proslogion* II from the reasoning of *Proslogion* III is not that the two Chapters represent two discrete and independent arguments or two different types of reasoning but rather that they represent two different types of existential claims about this being which are deducible from the fact that the being is that-than-which-a-greater-cannot-be-thought. What distinguishes the reasoning of *Proslogion* II from the reasoning of *Proslogion* III is that Chapter II represents the deduction that the being exists and Chapter III represents deductions about the nature of the existence of this being. In each case the deduction of the claim in question follows from the fact that if the claim is not true of the being than-which-a-greater-cannot-be-thought, then the being than-which-a-greater-cannot-be-thought is *not* the being than-which-a-greater-cannot-be-thought.

In *Proslogion* II Anselm deduces claim (c) that the being than-which-a-greater-cannot-be-thought exists by showing that, given certain principles about the relationship of thought to reality, then either (c) is true or

(B) the being than-which-a-greater-cannot-be-thought is *not* the being than-which-a-greater-cannot-be-thought

is true. In *Proslogion* III Anselm deduces claim (d), that the being than-which-a-greater-cannot-be-thought cannot be thought not to exist; and, as I shall try to show in my next chapter, Anselm deduces claim (e), that the being than-which-a-greater-cannot-be-thought cannot not exist, by showing that, given certain principles about the relationship of thought to reality, then either (d) and (e) are both true or (B) is true. In the chapters subsequent to *Proslogion* IV Anselm similarly deduces a series of claims which when taken together imply the claim (a′), that the being than-which-a-greater-cannot-be-thought bears the properties traditionally attributed to God. In *Proslogion* V Anselm deduces claim

(f) the being than-which-a-greater-cannot-be-thought is the supreme being existing through itself alone

and generalizes on the attributes of this being by deducing the general claim

(g) the being than-which-a-greater-cannot-be-thought is whatever it is better to be than not to be

from which he immediately deduces that the being is truthful and happy and from which he subsequently deduces in Chapter VI that the being is perceptive, omnipotent, merciful, and impassible, and in subsequent chapters that the being has further theistic attributes by showing that, given certain principles about the relationship of thought to reality, then either (f) and (g) and everything implied by (g) is true or (B) is true.

Certainly this procedure suggests the possibility of finding in the *Proslogion* one set of principles about the relationship of thought to reality such that the reasoning for each claim represents not a complete and independent argument but rather a single step in a series of deductions of one single argument. The possibility of finding such a set of principles, then, suggests the possibility of interpreting *Proslogion* II and *Proslogion* III not as separate and independent arguments but rather as steps in the series of deductions of one single argument.

Summary

Earlier in this chapter I said that the primary concern of this discussion is to show, by an internal examination and analysis of the reasoning in *Proslogion* II and III and the subsequent commentary in the *Reply*, that *Proslogion* II and *Proslogion* III do not separately contain logically complete arguments for the existence of God but rather that the two Chapters have to be taken together and that together they form the basis for a series of deductions about the existence of a being minimally characterized as that-than-which-a-greater-cannot-be-thought. What I have subsequently shown is that the interpretation which will result from the proposed analysis and examination of the internal structure of the reasoning of these two Chapters is also suggested by an external analysis of Anselm's overall program and procedure in the *Proslogion* as a whole, both as that program is announced in the *Preface* and as it is in fact carried out. The result of examining his announced program was that Anselm's intention was seen to be to provide one single argument to prove whatever is believed about the Divine Being.

We saw that the current interpretations provide no justification for supposing that Anselm's actual procedure fails to correspond to his announced procedure of providing one single argument. In addition we saw that there is no one chapter nor any two chapters which could be taken together that could be treated as an argument to prove whatever is believed about the Divine Being. Hence, on the basis of Anselm's announced program, a third interpretation is possible which would treat the entire *Proslogion* as Anselm's one single argument where *Proslogion* II and *Proslogion* III represent several existential deductions in a series of deductions about the being than-which-a-greater-cannot-be-thought such that all the deductions taken together constitute whatever is believed about the Divine Being.

Next we saw that there was nothing in Anselm's actual procedure that was inconsistent with his announced procedure. This was shown by examining the treatments of the current interpretations whose adequacy would imply an inconsistency between Anselm's actual procedure and his announced procedure. The current interpretations which treat *Proslogion* II or *Proslogion* II and III as arguments for the existence of God turned out to be inadequate interpretations of these two Chapters on the grounds that Anselm does not purport in either of these Chapters to establish that God exists where the proposition "God exists" is taken to mean "the being bearing the properties traditionally attributed to God exists." It was shown that in Anselm's actual procedure it is the entire *Proslogion* that is intended to establish the claim that God exists and that, insofar as this is the case, his actual procedure corresponds to his announced procedure.

While it could not be definitively established that Anselm did not intend *Proslogion* II or *Proslogion* III to represent separate and logically complete arguments for some claim or other, it was argued that the assumption is at least rendered questionable by the fact that treating them as arguments for the existence of God is inadequate.

Furthermore, it was observed that treating these Chapters as separate and independent arguments is never justified by commentators and that Anselm's procedure for establishing the several claims suggests the possibility of interpreting the reasoning in the various chapters as deductions from one set of premises such that all of the deductions taken together imply the claim that God exists or, alternatively, that all of the deductions taken together constitute whatever is believed about the Divine Being. Hence, on the basis of Anselm's actual procedure in the *Proslogion*, a third interpretation is possible which would treat the entire *Proslogion* as Anselm's one single argument where *Proslogion* II and *Proslogion* III represent several existential deductions in a series of deductions about the being than-which-a-greater-cannot-be-thought such that from all the deductions taken together the proposition that God exists is deducible.

In my next chapter I will try to show, by the proposed internal examination and analysis of the reasoning both in *Proslogion* II and III and in the subsequent commentary on these two Chapters in the *Reply* and by examining the analysis of this reasoning given both by the traditional and by the new interpretations, that *Proslogion* II and *Proslogion* III do not separately contain logically complete arguments for the existence of God but rather that the two Chapters have to be taken together and that together they form the basis for a series of deductions about the existence of a being minimally characterized as that-than-which-a-greater-cannot-be-thought.

CHAPTER TWO

ANSELM'S PROGRAM IN *PROSLOGION* II AND *PROSLOGION* III

In the previous chapter I tried to show that Anselm's overall program or procedure in the *Proslogion*, both as it is announced in the *Preface* and as it is in fact carried out, suggests a plausible third or alternative interpretation of the reasoning in and the relationship between *Proslogion* II and *Proslogion* III. This third or alternative interpretation is distinguished from the traditional interpretation and the new interpretation in that it treats the entire *Proslogion* as Anselm's argument for the existence of God rather than treating *Proslogion* II or *Proslogion* III or both as complete and independent arguments for the existence of God. On the basis of Anselm's overall procedure, the third or alternative interpretation differs from the other interpretations by treating *Proslogion* II and *Proslogion* III as dependent steps in a series of deductions whose ultimate conclusion is that God exists. Insofar as *Proslogion* II and III can be treated in isolation from the remainder of the *Proslogion*, this third or alternative interpretation treats these two Chapters as representing the basis for a series of existential deductions about the being than-which-a-greater-cannot-be-thought. My present chapter is devoted to the treatment of *Proslogion* II and III in isolation from the remainder of the *Proslogion* as these two Chapters are customarily treated. I will try to show that even in isolation an analysis of the internal structure of *Proslogion* II and III suggests the third or alternative interpretation when that analysis is guided by both Anselm's subsequent commentary on these two Chapters in the *Reply*, and a comparison of the current interpretations with the reasoning of *Proslogion* II and III.

What Anselm Purports to Establish
In Proslogion II and Proslogion III

Even when we consider *Proslogion* II and III by themselves, the unsupported assumption of the current interpretations that Anselm purports to establish, in these two Chapters alone, the claim that God exists is subject to some of the same criticisms which were argued for in my first chapter. In both *Proslogion* II and *Proslogion* III the subject of the reasoning is the being than-which-a-greater-cannot-be-thought. No matter how the reasoning of these two Chapters is to be identified or characterized the reasoning is about this being and not about God. At the end of *Proslogion* II Anselm says

> Therefore there is absolutely no doubt that something-than-which-a-greater-cannot-be-thought exists both in the mind and in reality[1].

The reasoning of *Proslogion* III begins and ends with the claim that *this being* exists so truly that it cannot even be thought not to exist. Nowhere in these two Chapters does Anselm *argue* that God exists in the mind and in reality or that God cannot even be thought not to exist. In these two Chapters the sole connection between the claims made about the being than-which-a-greater-cannot-be-thought and any claims that could be made about God consists in Anselm's assertion (a) that God is this being. The assumption that either *Proslogion* II or *Proslogion* III alone are intended by Anselm to establish that God exists rests on the assumption that Anselm intended his assertion (a) to function in *Proslogion* II or *Proslogion* III alone as a justification for the application of claims established about the being than-which-a-greater-cannot-be-thought to God.

Leaving aside, for the moment, the question of Anselm's intentions, his assertion (a) does not function adequately in *Proslogion* II and III as a justification for the application, to God, of claims established about the being than-which-a-greater-cannot-be-thought; and, hence, neither of these Chapters *does* establish that God exists. Even if we grant that certain claims about the being than-which-a-greater-cannot-be-thought are established there, it does not follow that they hold true of God; that is, they are not established to hold true of God unless assertion (a) functions as a justification for the application to God of claims established about the being than-which-a-greater-cannot-be-thought either by virtue of the fact that assertion (a) is a definition or by virtue of the fact that assertion (a) is itself established. If (a) is a definition then it is not required that (a) be established, and it is true that (G) is established by virtue of the fact that (a) is a definition if (c) is established.

However, if (a) is a definition then while it serves as a justification

---

[1] Anselm, *St. Anselm's Proslogion with a Reply on Behalf of the Fool by Gaunilo and the Author's Reply to Gaunilo*, trans. with an introduction and philosophical commentary by M. J. Charlesworth (Oxford: Clarendon Press, 1965), p. 117.

for the application of claims established about the being than-which-a-greater-cannot-be-thought to God, the conclusions derived on the basis of this justification are trivially true and have no more religious significance than the claims already established about the being than-which-a-greater-cannot-be-thought. The reason for this is that if (a) is a definition, then assertions about God are equivalent in meaning to corresponding assertions about the being than-which-a-greater-cannot-be-thought. So if (G) is established from (c) by invoking (a) as a justification and (a) is a definition, then (G) is equivalent in meaning to (c). Consequently, if (c) is established and is in fact true, then (G) is trivially true and has no more religious significance than (c) because (G) means (c). But while it is true that if (a) is a definition then (G) is established in *Proslogion* II or III where (G) means (c), it is not the case that (a) functions in *Proslogion* II and III as an adequate justification to establish the far more religiously significant claim (G') that the being bearing the properties traditionally attributed to God exists.

Now surely the question of whether or not God exists is equivalent in meaning to the question of whether or not the being bearing the properties traditionally attributed to God exists and is *not equivalent* in meaning to the question of whether or not the being than-which-a-greater-cannot-be-thought exists. If (a) is a definition then surely *Proslogion* II and III do not even address themselves to the question of whether or not God exists where the question has any religiously significant sense over, above, and beyond the question of whether or not the being than-which-a-greater-cannot-be-thought exists. Consequently, if (a) is a definition, then *Proslogion* II and III establish (G) where (G) means (c) if they establish (c), but these two Chapters do not establish (G) where (G) means (G'). Accordingly, since (a) is not a religiously significant definition it follows that if (a) is a definition, then neither *Proslogion* II nor *Proslogion* III establishes the existence of God in any religiously significant sense even if (c) is established in these two Chapters.

Since (a) does not function adequately as a justification for the application of claims established about the being than-which-a-greater-cannot-be-thought to God when (a) is treated as a definition, (a) does not function adequately as such a justification in *Proslogion* II and III unless (a) is independently established. If (a) were established then it would be established that claims true of the being than-which-a-greater-cannot-be-thought are also true of God. Hence, if *Proslogion* II or III establish (c) then if (a) were established independently in these Chapters, then (G) would be established in *Proslogion* II or III or both. Without such a proof for (a) it is possible to consistently hold that the being in question exists and that Anselm has established that the being exists and still deny both that God exists and that Anselm has established that God exists. In other words, it is not in the least obviously inconsistent to grant the truth of (c) and deny the truth of (a) because in the same way that (c) is not self-evident and needs to be established, neither is (a) self-evident, it also needs to be established.

Consequently, if *Proslogion* II or *Proslogion* III or both establish (G) in any religiously significant sense, then (a) is established in these two Chapters independently of (c). Since (a) is not established in these two Chapters, then neither *Proslogion* II nor *Proslogion* III establishes (G). It follows, then, since (a) is not a religiously significant definition and since (a) is not established in either *Proslogion* II or III, that (a) does not function as an adequate justification for the application of claims established about the being than-which-a-greater-cannot-be-thought to God and it follows that neither *Proslogion* II nor *Proslogion* III establishes the existence of God in any religiously significant sense even if (c) is established in these two Chapters.

It is true that the preceding arguments show only that Anselm did not establish the existence of God in *Proslogion* II and III. These arguments do not prove that Anselm did not intend to establish the existence of God in these two Chapters. Nevertheless, these arguments certainly do suggest the possibility that Anselm did not intend to establish the existence of God in *Proslogion* II and III, because if Anselm intended to establish the existence of God in *Proslogion* II and III, then he intended that assertion (a) be an adequate justification for the application of claims established about the being than-which-a-greater-cannot-be-thought to God. Now the fact that (a) does not function adequately as such a justification does not lead simply to the one conclusion that Anselm intended to establish the existence of God in *Proslogion* II and III alone and failed.

The fact that (a) does not function adequately as such a justification leads to *two* possible conclusions. Either Anselm intended to establish the existence of God in *Proslogion* II and III alone and failed because he intended that (a) function as an adequate justification and it does not, or Anselm did not intend to establish the existence of God in *Proslogion* II and III alone because he did not intend that assertion (a) function as such a justification. Accordingly, both the fact that the claim that Anselm intended to establish the existence of God in *Proslogion* II or III reduces to the claim that Anselm intended that assertion (a) function in these two Chapters as such a justification, and the fact that (a) does not function adequately as such a justification raises the possibility that Anselm never intended to establish the existence of God in *Proslogion* II or III. Whether or not Anselm intended to establish (G) in these two Chapters alone depends upon whether or not Anselm intended that assertion (a) function there as a justification for the application, to God, of claims established about the being than-which-a-greater-cannot-be-thought.

One of the odd features of the current interpretations is that the proponents of these interpretations always simply assume that assertion (a) is intended by Anselm to function as such a justification in *Proslogion* II and III, and they always either assume or state explicitly that (a) is intended by Anselm to be a definition. Not one proponent of the current interpretations even tries to argue for the position or give a reason for assuming that (a) was intended by Anselm to be a definition. Another odd feature of the current interpretations is that the proponents of these interpretations rarely go beyond the scope of *Proslogion* II and III in their analysis of the *Proslogion*. As I tried to show in my first chapter, if we go beyond the scope of *Proslogion* II and III, there is good reason to think that Anselm intended to establish only a certain set of claims about the being than which a greater cannot be thought and that he did not intend to establish (G) and, hence, that he did not intend that (a) function in these two Chapters as a justification for the application, to God, of claims established about the being than-which-a-greater-cannot-be-thought. But even if we remain within the scope of *Proslogion* II and III and the subsequent commentary on these two Chapters which constitute the *Reply*, the assumption that Anselm intended that assertion (a) function as such a justification presumably has as its sole reason the fact that Anselm asserts (a) in *Proslogion* II and III.

I know of no other reason for such an assumption. Both defender and critic alike assume that assertion (a) was intended by Anselm to function as such a justification without ever giving any reason for such an assumption. So presumably the fact that (a) occurs in *Proslogion* II and III constitutes the reason for that assumption. Consequently, the decision of whether assertion (a) is more accurately interpreted as Anselm's intention to provide such a justification and, hence, whether *Proslogion* II and III were intended by Anselm to establish (G) or whether it is more accurate *not* to interpret (a) as Anselm's intention to provide such a justification and, hence, whether *Proslogion* II and III were *not* intended by Anselm to establish (G) depends upon what *Proslogion* II and III and the *Reply* suggest about the status of assertion (a).

If we carefully examine assertion (a) as it occurs in *Proslogion* II and III and consult Anselm's further remarks in the *Reply* that are relevant to this issue, then even without invoking as evidence what Anselm says or the way he proceeds in the subsequent chapters of the *Proslogion* itself, we find that it is not at all obvious that Anselm intended that assertion (a) function in *Proslogion* II and III alone as a justification for the application, to God, of claims established about the being than-which-a-greater-cannot-be-thought or that he intended to establish (G) in these two Chapters alone. Rather, such an examination suggests that the most Anselm is attempting to do in *Proslogion* II and III is to establish a certain set of existential claims about the being than-which-a-greater-cannot-be-thought.

When we examine the occurrences of assertion (a) in *Proslogion* II and III we find that (a) occurs twice, once in each Chapter. In both cases the assertion occurs outside the scope of the reasoning about the being than-which-a-greater-cannot-be-thought. Its first occurrence is in the introductory portion of *Proslogion* II and is explicitly stated as a *belief* about the nature of God. Anselm says, "Now we believe that You are something than which nothing greater can be thought." [2] Nowhere else in *Proslogion* II does this assertion occur, nor does Anselm indicate in any way that assertion (a) has any status other than a belief. In fact assertion (a) seems to have only one function in this Chapter.

Expressed simply as a belief this assertion functions to introduce the main question to which Anselm is going to address himself in *Proslogion* II, namely, "can it be that a thing of such a nature does not exist?" [3] Explicitly what Anselm is asking is: can it be that the being than-which-a-greater-cannot-be-thought does not exist? This

---
[2] Ibid.
[3] Ibid.

question Anselm subsequently answers by purporting to establish in the entire remainder of *Proslogion* II that the being than-which-a-greater-cannot-be-thought *does* exist. The question arises out of two conflicting beliefs: the belief of the Fool that God does *not* exist and the belief of Anselm that God is that-than-which-a-greater-cannot-be-thought. Now if the Fool is correct in his belief and if Anselm is correct in his belief, then God does not exist and God is that-than-which-a-greater-cannot-be-thought. If both Anselm and the Fool are correct, then it follows that the being than-which-a-greater-cannot-be-thought does *not* exist. Hence, if it can be established that this being *does* exist it follows not that God exists, but rather it follows that either God exists or God is not the being in question.

In other words, if it is established that the being in question *does* exist, then it is established that either the Fool is wrong in his belief or Anselm is wrong in his belief. Hence if it is established that the being in question does exist then it follows that God exists *if God is the being in question*. But is God the being in question? Is assertion (a) true? Obviously if one believes assertion (a) and accepts (c) as established in *Proslogion* II, then one is committed to believing (G). Anselm, for example, is such a person. But surely the fact that Anselm believes (a) neither makes (a) true, nor does it oblige the Fool or anyone else to believe (a) or accept (a) as true. Assertion (a) does not have any peculiar status which guarantees its truth. It is perfectly consistent to accept (c) as established in *Proslogion* II and deny the truth of (G) so long as the truth of (a) is also denied. However, the question before us is whether or not Anselm intended to establish (G) in *Proslogion* II and III and, hence, whether or not Anselm intended (a) to function in *Proslogion* II and III as a justification for the application, to God, of claims established about the being than-which-a-greater-cannot-be-thought.

Consequently, the important question is: did Anselm think that it is inconsistent to accept (c) as established and deny the truth of (G)? If Anselm thinks that it is inconsistent to accept (c) as established in *Proslogion* II or III and deny the truth of (G), then it must be on the grounds that Anselm intended (a) to function as a self-evident justification for the application, to God, of claims established about the being than-which-a-greater-cannot-be-thought and, hence, it must be true that Anselm intended to establish (G) in *Proslogion* II or III alone. If Anselm thinks that it is not inconsistent to accept (c) as established in *Proslogion* II or III and deny the truth of (G), then it must be on the grounds that Anselm did *not* intend (a) to function as a self-evident justification for the application, to God, of claims established about the being than-which-a-greater-cannot-be-thought; and, hence, it must be true that Anselm did *not* intend to establish (G) in *Proslogion* II or III alone.

But there is nothing in either *Proslogion* II or *Proslogion* III to indicate that Anselm thinks that it is inconsistent to accept (c) as established and deny the truth of (G) and there is only indirect evidence in *Proslogion* II and III to indicate that Anselm thinks that it is *not* inconsistent to accept (c) as established and deny the truth of (G). In *Proslogion* II assertion (a) occurs only once, and that occurrence of (a) is in the introductory portion of the Chapter. Beyond the simple fact that (a) is asserted in *Proslogion* II, there is nothing in the remainder of *Proslogion* II to suggest that Anselm thinks that it is inconsistent to accept (c) as established and deny the truth of (G), and there is a very good reason for this which is consistent with the idea that Anselm did not intend to establish (G) in this Chapter. The remainder of *Proslogion* II is *entirely* devoted to establishing (c). Surely the fact that the remainder of *Proslogion* II is entirely devoted to establishing (c) suggests that Anselm did not intend to establish (G); surely it suggests that Anselm's primary concern in *Proslogion* II was simply to establish (c) and that (a) was not intended to function as a self-evident justification for the application of claims established about the being than-which-a-greater-cannot-be-thought to God, but rather that (a) was intended only to raise the question for which the remainder of *Proslogion* II provides an answer. From what Anselm says in *Proslogion* II there is no reason to suppose that he thinks that it is inconsistent to accept (c) as established and deny the truth of (G) and there is some reason to suppose that Anselm is only attempting to establish (c) in *Proslogion* II.

The second occurrence of assertion (a) in these two Chapters is in *Proslogion* III. In *Proslogion* III assertion (a) occurs *after* the reasoning which is presumably intended to establish that the being than-which-a-greater-cannot-be-thought exists so truly that it cannot be thought not to exist. Anselm says:

> And You, Lord our God, are this being. You exist so truly, Lord my God, that You cannot even be thought not to exist.[4]

---

[4] *Ibid.*, p. 119.

Even here there is no reason to suppose that Anselm thinks that it is inconsistent to accept as established that the being than-which-a-greater-cannot-be-thought exists so truly that it cannot be thought not to exist and to deny that God exists so truly that He cannot be thought not to exist. There is no reason to suppose that Anselm regards assertion (a) as it occurs in *Proslogion* III as anything more than an assertion of his belief about the nature of God such that if the belief is true, then God exists so truly that He cannot be thought not to exist. It is important to notice that Anselm does not use assertion (a) in the passage quoted above as a justification to move from the presumably established claim that the being than-which-a-greater-cannot-be-thought exists so truly that it cannot be thought not to exist to the claim that God exists so truly that He cannot be thought not to exist. Anselm asserts that God exists so truly that He cannot be thought not to exist and he asserts this because of (a), but there is a complete absence of any of the typical Anselmian conclusion-language which would indicate that the proposition about God is intended to follow from the proposition about the being than-which-a-greater-cannot-be-thought and assertion (a). Rather, the proposition about God is asserted as a belief that Anselm is committed to by virtue of the fact that he believes (a) and has established that the being than-which-a-greater-cannot-be-thought exists so truly that it cannot be thought not to exist.

In fact the structure of *Proslogion* III suggests that Anselm is attempting to establish only that the being than-which-a-greater-cannot-be-thought exists so truly that it cannot be thought not to exist, and what suggests this is the fact that Anselm does not use assertion (a) as a justification for the application of the claim established about the being than-which-a-greater-cannot-be-thought to God. From what Anselm says in *Proslogion* III there is no reason to suppose that he thinks that it is inconsistent to accept claims established about the being than-which-a-greater-cannot-be-thought and to deny the truth of corresponding claims about God and there is some reason to suppose that Anselm is only attempting to establish in *Proslogion* III that the being than-which-a-greater-cannot-be-thought exists so truly that it cannot be thought not to exist.

In short, neither *Proslogion* II nor *Proslogion* III provides any reason to suppose that Anselm thinks that it is inconsistent to accept as established claims about the being than-which-a-greater-cannot-be-thought and to deny the truth of corresponding claims about God.

Consequently neither *Proslogion* II nor *Proslogion* III provides any reason to suppose that Anselm intended (a) to function as a justification for the application of claims established about the being than-which-a-greater-cannot-be-thought to God, and, hence, they do not provide any reason to suppose that Anselm was attempting to establish (G) in these two Chapters alone. Moreover, both *Proslogion* II and *Proslogion* III do provide some reason for supposing that Anselm did not intend assertion (a) to function as a self-evident justification for the application of claims established about the being than-which-a-greater-cannot-be-thought to God, and, hence, they do provide some reason for supposing that Anselm was not attempting to establish (G) in these two Chapters alone.

But while there is no conclusive evidence in either *Proslogion* II or *Proslogion* III for deciding whether or not Anselm thinks that it is inconsistent to accept as established claims about the being than-which-a-greater-cannot-be-thought and to deny the truth of corresponding claims about God, there is conclusive evidence in the *Reply*. In Chapter VII of the *Reply* Anselm states explicitly that denying claims about God is not sufficient grounds for denying corresponding claims about the being than-which-a-greater-cannot-be-thought. Anselm says:

> For is it reasonable that someone should therefore *deny what he understands because it is said to be [the same as] that which he denies since he does not understand it?* ... For this reason it cannot be believed that anyone should deny 'that-than-which-a-greater-cannot-be-thought' (which, being heard, he understands to some extent), on the ground that he denies God whose meaning he does not think of in any way at all.[5] (Italics mine.)

Anselm is saying two things here. He explicitly states that denying claims about God is not sufficient grounds for denying corresponding claims about the being than-which-a-greater-cannot-be-thought and he explicitly states that assertion (a) does not provide a justification for denying claims about the being than-which-a-greater-cannot-be-thought for anyone denying corresponding claims about God. In other words, Anselm makes it quite clear both that he does *not* think that it is inconsistent to accept (c) as established and to deny the truth of (G) and that he does *not* regard (a) as a self-evident

---

[5] *Ibid.*, p. 185.

justification for the application of claims established about the being than-which-a-greater-cannot-be-thought to God.

Since Anselm does not think that it is inconsistent to accept as established claims about the being than-which-a-greater-cannot-be-thought and to deny corresponding claims about God and since Anselm does not regard assertion (a) as a self-evident justification for the application of claims established about the being than-which-a-greater-cannot-be-thought to God, there is no reason to suppose that Anselm intended to establish (G) or any claims about God in *Proslogion* II or III. There is no reason to suppose that Anselm was trying to do any more than to establish a certain set of existential claims about the being than-which-a-greater-cannot-be-thought in these two Chapters. Not only is the assumption of the current interpretations that Anselm was attempting to establish (G) in one or both of these two Chapters alone unsupported, the evidence suggests that the assumption is false. From what Anselm says in *Proslogion* II, *Proslogion* III, and the *Reply*, it is more accurate not to interpret *Proslogion* II or III as Anselm's attempt to establish (G). Rather, it is more accurate to interpret *Proslogion* II and III as Anselm's attempt to establish a certain set of existential claims about the being than-which-a-greater-cannot-be-thought.

The Reply and Anselm's Single-Argument Claim

In fact, it is the being than-which-a-greater-cannot-be-thought and not God that is the actual subject of the *Proslogion*. The claims Anselm purports to establish are claims about this being and not about God. The truth of the claim that God exists issues not from the fact that Anselm argues that the being traditionally referred to as God exists. Rather, the truth of the claim that God exists is a consequence of the fact that Anselm provides one single argument (not about God but about the being than-which-a-greater-cannot-be-thought) in which he deduces both that the being than-which-a-greater-cannot-be-thought exists and that the being than-which-a-greater-cannot-be-thought bears the properties traditionally attributed to God. It is not even necessary to go beyond the scope of *Proslogion* II, *Proslogion* III, and the *Reply* to see that this is Anselm's intention.

In Chapter X of the *Reply* Anselm's concluding remarks reveal that this is his intention in the *Proslogion*. Anselm says:

> I think now that I have shown that I have proved in the above tract, not

by a weak argumentation but by a sufficiently necessary one, *that something-than-which-a-greater-cannot-be-thought exists in reality itself*, and that *this proof* has not been weakened by the force of any objection. For the import of *this proof* is in itself of such force that *what is spoken of is proved* (as a necessary consequence of the fact that it is understood or thought of) *both to exist in actual reality and to be itself whatever must be believed about the Divine Being*. For we believe of the Divine Being whatever it can, absolutely speaking, be thought better to be than not to be. For example, it is better to be eternal than not eternal, good than not good, indeed goodness-itself than not goodness-itself. However, nothing of this kind cannot but be that-than-which-a-greater-cannot-be-thought. *It is, then, necessary that 'that-than-which-a-greater-cannot-be-thought' should be whatever must be believed about the Divine Nature.*[6] (Italics mine.)

In this passage Anselm gives a synopsis of what he has done in the *Proslogion*. First he claims that in the *Proslogion* he has proved the existence of the being than-which-a-greater-cannot-be-thought. This is obviously a reference to the reasoning in the *Proslogion* II-*Proslogion* III complex where Anselm in fact attempts to establish only a certain set of existential claims about the being than-which-a-greater-cannot-be-thought. It is important to notice that Anselm does not claim in this passage to have established the existence of God in the *Proslogion*. In fact, just as in the *Proslogion* itself, the subject of this synopsis is not God but the being than-which-a-greater-cannot-be-thought. In this passage Anselm makes it quite clear that God's existence is established by providing one proof about the being than-which-a-greater-cannot-be-thought. That proof is not one which establishes the existence of God by invoking assertion (a) as a definition. Rather, God's existence is established in the proof as a necessary consequence of the fact that it is deducible both that the being than-which-a-greater-cannot-be-thought exists and that the being than-which-a-greater-cannot-be-thought is itself whatever must be believed about the Divine Being.

In other words, God's existence is not established by deducing that the being exists and then stipulating, or guessing, or believing, or simply asserting that the being is God. Instead, God's existence is established by deducing that the being exists and by deducing, establishing, that the being is God. Surely, then, neither *Proslogion* II nor *Proslogion* III was intended by Anselm to establish the existence

---

[6] *Ibid.*, pp. 189-191.

of God. In neither of these two Chapters does Anselm attempt to do more than deduce certain existential claims about the being than-which-a-greater-cannot-be-thought. In neither of these two Chapters does Anselm attempt to show that the being than-which-a-greater-cannot-be-thought is itself *whatever* must be believed about the Divine Being *except* that it exists and that its existence has certain attributes. Accordingly, Anselm did not intend that *Proslogion* II and III alone should establish the existence of God and the current interpretations misrepresent these two Chapters both by characterizing them and by treating them as arguments for the existence of God.

But the current interpretations not only treat *Proslogion* II and *Proslogion* III as Anselm's attempt at establishing the existence of God, the current interpretations also treat *Proslogion* II and *Proslogion* III as complete and independent arguments. We have already seen that *Proslogion* II and III are intended by Anselm to represent the deduction of a certain set of existential claims about the being than-which-a-greater-cannot-be-thought and that the subsequent chapters of the *Proslogion* are intended by Anselm to represent the deduction of a certain set of theistic claims about the being than-which-a-greater-cannot-be-thought. The question now is did Anselm intend that these existential deductions represent an argument complete and independent from the theistic deductions and did Anselm intend that these several existential deductions represent arguments complete and independent of one another?

The second point in the above quoted passage which Anselm makes quite clear about the *Proslogion* is that it contains *one proof* and the force of that proof is that both the existential claims and the theistic claims about the being than-which-a-greater-cannot-be-thought are deducible. From what Anselm says in Chapter X of the *Reply*, he does not regard each deduction as a complete and independent argument. Rather, for Anselm it is the entire *Proslogion* that constitutes his single argument where each section of the *Proslogion* represents a deductive step in that one single proof. Consequently, for Anselm the reasoning of *Proslogion* II and III represents a set of existential deductions in a series of deductions about the being than-which-a-greater-cannot-be-thought.

The result of examining *Proslogion* II, *Proslogion* III, and the *Reply* suggests that the third or alternative interpretation is more faithful to Anselm's intentions than the other interpretations, at least insofar as the third interpretation treats "the being than-which-a-greater-cannot-be-thought" and not "God" as the subject of *Proslogion* II and III. Such an examination indicates that Anselm did not intend to establish the existence of God in *Proslogion* II and III alone, but, rather, that examination indicates that all Anselm was trying to do in *Proslogion* II and III was to establish the existence and something about the existence of the being than-which-a-greater-cannot-be-thought. Furthermore, the third or alternative interpretation is further substantiated by the fact that Chapter X of the *Reply* strongly indicates that neither *Proslogion* II nor *Proslogion* III is intended by Anselm to be a logically complete and independent argument.

Chapter X of the *Reply* indicates that *Proslogion* II and *Proslogion* III are not intended by Anselm to be either independent of one another or of the remainder of the *Proslogion*, instead it indicates that *Proslogion* II and *Proslogion* III represent several deductions in a series of deductions in one proof. But since it is possible that the proponents of the current interpretations could be correct in treating *Proslogion* II or *Proslogion* II and III as logically complete and independent arguments even though they are wrong in treating these two Chapters as arguments for the existence of God, it is necessary to examine the reasoning of *Proslogion* II and *Proslogion* III in which Anselm purports to establish his existential claims about the being than-which-a-greater-cannot-be-thought in order to see if what Anselm claims in Chapter X of the *Reply* about the relationship of these two Chapters actually obtains. Although it is not very likely, it is possible that Anselm intended that these two Chapters have some relationship when in fact they are complete and independent arguments for the existence of the being than-which-a-greater-cannot-be-thought.

Consequently, insofar as it is possible to treat *Proslogion* II and III in isolation from the remainder of the *Proslogion*, the task remains both to compare *Proslogion* II, *Proslogion* III, and the *Reply* with the current interpretations of these Chapters in order to see that the arguments identified in these interpretations are not arguments that can be attributed to Anselm, and to examine in detail *Proslogion* II, *Proslogion* III, and the *Reply* in order to determine precisely what is the reasoning in and the relationship between *Proslogion* II and *Proslogion* III. I will begin this task by first comparing the new interpretation with *Proslogion* III and the *Reply* in order to show that

Proslogion III cannot be interpreted as containing any logically complete and independent argument which can be attributed to Anselm. Subsequently, by comparing the current interpretations with *Proslogion* II and the *Reply*, I will argue that *Proslogion* II cannot be interpreted as containing any logically complete and independent argument which can be attributed to Anselm.

But before I begin, it will help in the task to make a minor adjustment in the current interpretations. If we correct the current interpretations with respect to what we have already discovered about the proper subject of *Proslogion* II and III by stipulating that in the analyses of *Proslogion* II and *Proslogion* III given by the current interpretations the occurrence of the word "God" is simply an abbreviation for the term "being than-which-a-greater-cannot-be-thought," in other words, if we stipulate that the word "God" is not intensionally equivalent to the term "being bearing the properties traditionally attributed to God," then we are in a position to examine in isolation that part of the analyses given by the current interpretations which treat *Proslogion* II or *Proslogion* III as complete and independent arguments without confusing it with that part of these analyses which treat these two Chapters as arguments for the existence of God (the being bearing the properties traditionally attributed to God). Such an isolation of the parts of the analyses given by the current interpretations is justified on the grounds that the actual reasoning about the being than-which-a-greater-cannot-be-thought in *Proslogion* II and *Proslogion* III is logically independent of assertion (a).

Consequently, the question of whether or not *Proslogion* II and III represent complete and independent arguments depends for its answer upon whether or not the reasoning about the being than-which-a-greater-cannot-be-thought represents complete and independent arguments. The question of whether or not *Proslogion* II and III represent arguments for the existence of God depends for its answer upon whether or not assertion (a) functions as an adequate justification for the application of claims established about the being than-which-a-greater-cannot-be-thought to God. Since the current interpretations treat *Proslogion* II and III as arguments for the existence of God only on the grounds that assertion (a) does function as such a justification, the claim that these two Chapters represent complete and independent arguments is logically independent of the claim that the arguments are about God. While the current interpretations are wrong in making the latter claim about *Proslogion* II and III, we want to see what *Proslogion* II, *Proslogion* III, and the *Reply* suggest with respect to the former claim about *Proslogion* II and III. For these reasons, then, we correct the current interpretations by stipulating that the word "God" is an *abbreviation* for the term "being than-which-a-greater-cannot-be-thought."

The Alleged Proslogion III Argument

According to the proponents of the new interpretation *Proslogion* II and *Proslogion* III each contain a logically complete and independent argument for the existence of God. On this view it is held that the *Proslogion* II argument fails because it rests on the assumption that existence is a predicate when in fact existence is not a predicate. But while the proponents of the new interpretation hold that there is a logically complete and independent argument in *Proslogion* II which attempts to establish the existence of God on the fallacious assumption that existence is a predicate, these proponents also claim that *Proslogion* III contains a different logically complete and independent argument which attempts to establish the claim that God *necessarily* exists where that claim implies that God exists: an argument which does not rest on the assumption that existence is a predicate.

Most of these proponents, notably Malcolm[7] and Charlesworth,[8] at one point or another in their analyses hedge on the question of whether or not Anselm regarded himself as offering two different proofs. They take it as obvious that Anselm regarded himself as offering a proof in *Proslogion* II but are not sure what his intentions were with respect to *Proslogion* III. Nevertheless, they conclude that in fact *Proslogion* II represents one logically complete and independent argument for the existence of God and that *Proslogion* III represents a different logically complete and independent argument for the existence of God no matter what Anselm's intentions were.

Presumably the possibility that Anselm did not intend that *Proslogion* III be a logically complete and independent argument is precluded by the fact that he did not in *Proslogion* II and III

---

[7] Norman Malcolm, "Anselm's Ontological Arguments," *Philosophical Review*, 69 (January, 1960), p. 41.

[8] Anselm, pp. 73-74.

explicitly assert his intentions on this issue (although he seems to be quite clear on this issue in Chapter X of the *Reply*) and by the fact that the proponents of the new interpretation are able to construct such an argument out of the assertions in *Proslogion* III. Since it is possible for a philosopher in the process of complex reasoning to give an argument he is not consciously aware of and one he did not particularly intend to provide, the evidence in Chapter X of the *Reply* does not provide any direct evidence to demonstrate that Anselm did not provide an argument in *Proslogion* III.

Similarly the simple fact that an argument can be constructed out of some of Anselm's remarks in *Proslogion* III does not provide conclusive evidence that Anselm provided such an argument either unconsciously or unintentionally. Whether or not Anselm provided an unintentional argument in *Proslogion* III depends upon whether or not Anselm's other intentions as they are expressed in the claims of *Proslogion* II, *Proslogion* III, and the *Reply* commit Anselm to the alleged argument which the proponents of the new interpretation identify. If Anselm's other remarks and claims do not commit him to the alleged *Proslogion* III argument, then it is difficult to understand how the alleged argument can be regarded as anything more than a representation of the views of the proponents of the new interpretation.

According to the proponents of the new interpretation, for example, Malcolm [9] and Charlesworth,[10] *Proslogion* III contains an argument which is intended to establish the claim (G2) that God necessarily exists where "necessarily" means logically necessary and where (G2) immediately implies (G). If *Proslogion* III does contain such an argument, then we would expect to find in *Proslogion* III both an argument and the conclusion (G2). But, as a matter of fact, we do not find (G2) as the conclusion in *Proslogion* III. Anselm's reasoning in *Proslogion* III is:

> And certainly this being so truly exists that it cannot be even thought not to exist. For something can be thought to exist that cannot be thought not to exist, and this is greater than that which can be thought not to exist. Hence, if that-than-which-a-greater-cannot-be-thought can be thought not to exist, then that-than-which-a-greater-cannot-be-thought is not the same as that-than-which-a-greater-cannot-be-

---

[9] Malcolm, p. 58.
[10] Anselm, p. 73.

thought, which is absurd. *Something-than-which-a-greater-cannot-be-thought exists so truly then, that it cannot be even thought not to exist.*[11] (Italics mine.)

If there is an argument at all here, then the conclusion of this argument is stated in the first sentence and is repeated again in the final sentence, but the conclusion is not assertion (G2). The closest we can come to finding an assertion anything nearly like (G2) would be in the denial of the antecedent of the third sentence. The antecedent of the third sentence is that-than-which-a-greater-cannot-be-thought *can* be thought not to exist *(potest cogitari non esse)*. The denial of this antecedent would be assertion (d) that that-than-which-a-greater-cannot-be-thought *cannot* be thought not to exist *(non potest cogitari non esse* or alternatively, for Anselm, *non possit cogitari non esse)*. But even if we convert Anselm's phrase *"non potest cogitari (non esse),"* literally translated as "cannot be thought (not to exist)," to "logically impossible (not to exist)" or "necessarily (exists)" as Malcolm [12] and Charlesworth [13] do, then while the denial of the antecedent of the third sentence would be equivalent to (G2), Anselm does not conclude his reasoning by deducing the denial of the antecedent of the third sentence as we would expect him to do if he intended this passage to constitute a logically complete and independent argument whose conclusion is (G2).

Instead Anselm concludes the reasoning in *Proslogion* III with the far more complex proposition that something-than-which-a-greater-cannot-be-thought exists so truly that it cannot be thought not to exist, and this proposition is not equivalent to (G2) even if we allow (G2) as a transformation of the denial of the antecedent in the third sentence because this concluding proposition is not equivalent to the denial of that antecedent. The denial of that antecedent, assertion (d), is simply the assertion that the being than-which-a-greater-cannot-be-thought cannot be thought not to exist. The concluding proposition of the *Proslogion* III reasoning is a much more complex assertion that Anselm is making about the being than-which-a-greater-cannot-be-thought. This proposition clearly makes at least two claims about the being which are presumably supposed to follow from what precedes the proposition (it is important to remember at

---

[11] Anselm, p. 119.
[12] Malcolm, p. 45.
[13] Anselm, p. 73.

this point that *Proslogion* II precedes this proposition as well as the reasoning of *Proslogion* III).

This proposition clearly asserts *both* that the being cannot be thought not to exist *and* that the being exists. But the proposition also makes a third claim. It asserts that the being exists *so truly* that it cannot be thought not to exist. The force of the phrase "so truly" in this proposition is that not only is it a fact that the being exists and not only is it a fact that the being cannot be thought not to exist but also that the being's existence corresponds to the fact that it cannot be thought not to exist, that is, that it cannot not exist. If there is any doubt that this is Anselm's meaning, we have only to consult the *Reply* where Anselm explicitly distinguishes these three claims from one another and indicates that each one is deducible in his proof. In Chapter V of the *Reply* Anselm says:

> Thus, if anyone should say that 'that-than-which-a-greater-cannot-be-thought' is not something that actually exists, or that it can possibly not exist, or even can be thought of as not existing, he can easily be refuted ... It is evident, then, that it neither does not exist nor can not exist or be thought of as not existing.[14]

In short, Anselm does not conclude his reasoning in *Proslogion* III by deducing assertion (d) from the third sentence as we would expect him to do if he intended *Proslogion* III to constitute a logically complete and independent argument whose conclusion is (G2). Rather, Anselm concludes the reasoning of *Proslogion* III with the far more complex proposition that the being than-which-a-greater-cannot-be-thought exists, cannot be thought not to exist, and cannot not exist, that is, the complex proposition (c)-(d)-(e). Even if we allow the transformation of (d) into (G2), the proposition with which Anselm concludes the reasoning of *Proslogion* III would not be (G2) but (c)-(G2)-(e). Of course, if it is true that Anselm concludes the reasoning of *Proslogion* III with (c)-(G2)-(e), then it is true that Anselm concludes the reasoning of *Proslogion* III with (G2). But while it may be true that Anselm concludes the reasoning of *Proslogion* III with (c)-(d)-(e) or (c)-(G2)-(e) and, hence, with (d) or (G2), Anselm by so concluding the reasoning of *Proslogion* III cannot be regarded as deducing (d) or (G2) from the reasoning of *Proslogion* III alone unless he is also regarded as deducing (c) and (e) from the reasoning of *Proslogion* III alone, because in concluding the

---

[14] Anselm, pp. 179-181.

reasoning of *Proslogion* III with (c)-(d)-(e) or (c)-(G2)-(e), Anselm is not only concluding the reasoning with (d) or (G2), but he is equally concluding the reasoning with (c) and (e) as well. In the proposition (c)-(d)-(e) or (c)-(G2)-(e) with which Anselm concludes the reasoning of *Proslogion* III, each component claim shares the same logical status with the other claims so that if Anselm intended to deduce any of these claims from the reasoning of *Proslogion* III alone, then there is no more reason to think that he intended to deduce (d) or (G2) from the reasoning of *Proslogion* III alone than there is to think that he intended to deduce (c) and (e) from the reasoning of *Proslogion* III alone. Consequently if *Proslogion* III represents a logically complete and independent argument, then the conclusion of the argument is not (G2) but (c)-(d)-(e) or (c)-(G2)-(e).

In short, we do not find the conclusion (G2) that we would expect to find from what the proponents of the new interpretation tell us about *Proslogion* III. But neither do we find a logically complete and independent argument as we would expect to find from what the proponents of the new interpretation tell us about *Proslogion* III. Even a cursory reading of the reasoning of *Proslogion* III should make it plain that the two sentences that would have to be the premises of this alleged argument are not strong enough to support the conclusion (c)-(G2)-(e).

However, the objection might be raised at this point that while (c)-(G2)-(e) is not directly deducible from the two premises of *Proslogion* III, it is indirectly deducible, and, hence, *Proslogion* III does represent a logically complete and independent argument whose conclusion is (c)-(G2)-(e). It might be argued that (G2) is directly deducible from the two premises and that (G2) implies (c) and (e). As a matter of fact the proponents of the new interpretation argue very much like this. They claim that (G2) is supposed to be deducible from the two premises and that (G2) implies (G), and since (G) is intensionally equivalent to (c), their claim reduces to the claim that (G2) implies (c). The only exception is that the proponents of the new interpretation do not isolate (e) so that it is hard to say how they would handle it, but if they are to maintain the view that *Proslogion* III represents a logically complete and independent argument they would have to provide some way of accounting for (e). But even if we grant that (G2) is deducible from *Proslogion* III and even if we grant the assumption that (G2) implies (c), (e) cannot be accounted for by claiming that (G2) implies (e) because it does not.

At first sight it certainly seems plausible enough to hold that "God necessarily exists" implies "God cannot not exist" on the grounds that "x necessarily exists" implies "x cannot not exist." But while it may be true that "x necessarily exists" implies "x cannot not exist," it is not true that (G2) implies (e) when we recall that (G2) is the result of transforming "cannot be thought not to exist" in (d) to "necessarily exists" and is not a substitution instance of "x necessarily exists." Surely "God cannot be thought not to exist" does not imply "God cannot not exist." Consequently (e) cannot be accounted for by claiming that (G2) implies (e), and since the premises of the reasoning of *Proslogion* III are not strong enough to support (c)-(G2)-(e), the view that *Proslogion* III represents a logically complete and independent argument fails in the absence of any way of accounting for (e). The presence of (e) in *Proslogion* III can only be accounted for by the fact that Anselm did not intend to provide a logically complete and independent argument in *Proslogion* III.

But the objection still might be raised that even if the presence of (e) in *Proslogion* III can only be accounted for by the fact that Anselm did not intend to provide a logically complete and independent argument in *Proslogion* III, that is, that Anselm did not intend to establish (c)-(G2)-(e) by *Proslogion* III alone, it does not follow that Anselm did not in fact provide, albeit unintentionally, a logically complete and independent argument for (G2) in *Proslogion* III alone. It might still be argued that the premises of *Proslogion* III do in fact constitute a logically complete and independent argument whose conclusion is (G2): an argument to which Anselm is committed by virtue of what he said in *Proslogion* III.

The response to this argument is that even if we grant that (G2) implies (c), it is false that (G2) is deducible from what would have to be the premises of the *Proslogion* III argument if the reasoning of *Proslogion* III represents a logically complete and independent argument. The assumption that (G2) is deducible from *Proslogion* III alone rests on the assumptions that (d) is deducible from *Proslogion* III alone and that Anselm's phrase "cannot be thought (not to exist)" is transformable into "logically impossible (not to exist)" or "necessarily (exists)" so that (d) is transformable into (G2) and any propositions implying (d) are transformable into propositions implying (G2). But even if it is true that (d) is deducible from *Proslogion* III alone, (G2) is not deducible from any part of the *Proslogion* in any way that would preserve an accurate representation of Anselm's intentions because there are crucial objections to transforming Anselm's phrase "cannot be thought (not to exist)" in the indicated way required to deduce (G2). These objections become clear when we see how the proponents of the new interpretation carry out the transformations.

Malcolm represents the alleged *Proslogion* III argument in the following way:

> Anselm is saying ... that *a being whose nonexistence is logically impossible is "greater" than a being whose nonexistence is logically possible* (and therefore that a being a greater than which cannot be conceived must be one whose nonexistence is logically impossible)...[15] (Italics mine.)

Although it is not precisely what Anselm says, Malcolm presumably reads the second sentence of *Proslogion* III as "a being that cannot be thought not to exist is greater than a being that can be thought not to exist," and the italicized portion of Malcolm's interpretation is presumably the result of transforming Anselm's phrase "cannot be thought not to exist" into the phrase "nonexistence is logically impossible" and Anselm's phrase "can be thought not to exist" into the phrase "nonexistence is logically possible." Later on Malcolm indicates that the phrase "nonexistence is logically impossible" is equivalent to the phrase "necessarily exists"[16] so presumably for Malcolm the phrase "nonexistence is logically possible" is equivalent to the phrase "contingently exists." Accordingly, Malcolm's interpretation of *Proslogion* III would substantially agree with Charlesworth's interpretation which is represented as follows:

> God, argues St. Anselm here, cannot exist in a contingent way, for to exist necessarily ... is *greater* than existing contingently; so that if 'that than which nothing greater can be thought' were to exist contingently it would not be as great as it would be if it existed necessarily, and so would not be, precisely, that than which nothing greater can be thought.[17]

Again, although it is not precisely what Anselm says, Charlesworth subsequently claims that the second sentence of *Proslogion* III contains the premise that "what cannot be thought not to exist is

---

[15] Malcolm, p. 45.
[16] Malcolm, p. 46.
[17] Anselm, p. 73.

greater than what can be thought not to exist," and Charlesworth claims that this premise is equivalent to "what exists necessarily is greater than what exists contingently."[18] So presumably the latter claim issues from the former claim by transforming Anselm's phrase "cannot be thought not to exist" into the phrase "necessarily exists" and Anselm's phrase "can be thought not to exist" into the phrase "contingently exists." In a footnote Charlesworth indicates that the phrase "necessarily exists" is equivalent to the phrase "logically impossible not to exist"[19] so presumably the phrase "contingently exists" is equivalent to the phrase "logically possible not to exist." Accordingly, Charlesworth's interpretation of *Proslogion* III is substantially equivalent to Malcolm's interpretation.

Both of these interpreters of Anselm identify a logically complete and independent argument in *Proslogion* III whose conclusion is that God necessarily exists. They both read the second sentence of *Proslogion* III in the same way, and they both allow the transformation of Anselm's phrase "cannot be thought not to exist" into either "logically impossible not to exist" or "necessarily exists" and the transformation of Anselm's phrase "can be thought not to exist" into either "logically possible not to exist" or "contingently exists." Furthermore, both of these interpreters *require* these transformations in order to support the claim that *Proslogion* III contains a logically complete and independent argument whose conclusion is (G2). Consequently the claim that *Proslogion* III contains a logically complete and independent argument whose conclusion is (G2), an argument to which Anselm is committed despite the fact that he did not intend to provide such an argument, reduces to the claim that Anselm is committed to the indicated transformations.

Unfortunately, no justification is ever given for thinking that Anselm is committed to those transformations. I can think of only two possible justifications for thinking that Anselm is committed to them. Either Anselm is committed to those transformations because what he says entails those transformations or those transformations represent the meaning of what Anselm intended to express, whether or not he consciously intended to provide a logically complete and independent argument in *Proslogion* III. However, there are crucial objections to both of these possible justifications.

---
[18] *Ibid.*
[19] *Ibid.*

The first possible justification for transforming Anselm's phrase "cannot be thought" (*non possit cogitari*) into "is logically impossible" would be difficult indeed to defend because it simply seems false that the two phrases mutually entail one another. While it is true that "x is logically impossible" entails "x cannot be thought" and, hence, that the Malcolm-Charlesworth premises entail the *alleged* Anselm premises, it is not at all self-evident that "x cannot be thought" entails "x is logically impossible" and, hence, that the alleged Anselm premises entail the Malcolm-Charlesworth premises. The first entailment obviously holds, because being logically possible is a condition of thought. But perhaps being logically possible is not the only condition of thought. Perhaps there are causal and psychological conditions of thought such that "x cannot be thought" might be true while "x is logically impossible" might be false. In order to maintain the view that Anselm is *logically* committed to these transformations, one would have to show that the second entailment holds.

The second possible justification for thinking that Anselm is committed to these transformations, namely, that these transformations represent the meaning of what Anselm intended to express despite the fact that he may not have consciously intended to provide a logically complete and independent argument in *Proslogion* III, is the most plausible and probably represents the unexpressed views of the proponents of the new interpretation. The problem with this justification is that when all the relevant evidence which can be brought to bear on this issue is taken together, it renders as highly unconvincing the view that these transformations represent the meaning of what Anselm intended to express; and, hence, it renders as highly unconvincing the view that Anselm, despite his intentions to the contrary, did provide a logically complete and independent argument in *Proslogion* III whose conclusion is (G2).

The first objection to these transformations as an adequate representation of Anselm's intentions was raised by Professor Matthews in a short article responding to Malcolm's interpretation of Anselm.[20] In fact, Matthews' article was the only one in a series of several articles which challenged Malcolm's paper on the grounds that it was not an adequate interpretation of Anselm. All the other commentators presumably accept the interpretation as a faithful

---

[20] Gareth B. Matthews, "On Conceivability in Anselm and Malcolm," *Philosophical Review*, 70 (January, 1961), pp. 110-111.

rendition of Anselm or at least are not concerned with the question of whether or not Anselm's views were accurately represented. Such indifference, it seems to me, accounts for the fact that philosophers are so ready to accept Anselm's *Proslogion* reasoning as substantially the "same" as other so-called "ontological arguments." In his article Matthews points out that Malcolm does not make a general policy of interpreting Anselm's "*posse cogitari*" in terms of logical possibility and that there is a good reason not to do so. In Chapter XV of the *Proslogion* Anselm says that God is "something greater than can be thought" and Matthews argues:

> Presumably Anselm means that God exceeds our powers of comprehension, not that God is greater than is logically possible (and therefore, presumably, logically impossible).[21]

The point, of course, is that Chapter XV of the *Proslogion* provides evidence to suggest that these transformations do not represent the meaning that Anselm intended to express in the original phrases. Now, if there is any doubt that "x is greater than is logically possible" ought to be rendered as "x is logically impossible" that doubt could only be raised on the ground that it is not at all clear that "x is greater than is logically possible" has any meaning at all. In either case, if Anselm is committed to these transformations, then he is committed either to the proposition "God is logically impossible" or the meaningless proposition "God is greater than is logically possible." Consequently, the assumption that such transformations are consistent with Anselm's intentions can be maintained in the face of Matthews' objection only if we are willing to allow that in Chapter XV Anselm intended either to assert that God is logically impossible or to put forward a meaningless statement, or if we are willing to allow that *Proslogion* III is a special case and only there ought we to perform such transformations.

To hold either the view that Anselm is asserting that God is logically impossible or the view that Anselm has put forward a meaningless statement would be ridiculous and would be tantamount to admitting that we will maintain, in the face of all evidence to the contrary, the view that Anselm in fact provided a logically complete and independent argument in *Proslogion* III whose conclusion is (G2). To hold the view that *Proslogion* III is a special case where such

---

[21] *Ibid.*, p. 110.

transformations ought to be performed is without justification and would be tantamount to simply stipulating that such transformations represent the meaning that Anselm intended to express and, hence, would be tantamount to simply stipulating that *Proslogion* III contains a logically complete and independent argument whose conclusion is (G2). But the question before us is not whether or not such stipulations can be made but whether or not these transformations do in fact represent Anselm's intentions in *Proslogion* III.

So far there is no reason to suppose that these transformations do represent Anselm's intentions and good reason to suppose that they do not. But the problem with the view that *Proslogion* III is a special case where such transformations ought to be performed is not simply that it is never justified. There are further objections to such transformations which would even preclude the possibility of treating *Proslogion* III as a special case.

We have already seen that the beginning sentence and the concluding sentence of the reasoning of *Proslogion* III is a complex proposition asserting (c)-(d)-(e). Chapter V of the *Reply* makes it quite clear that Anselm *intends* to distinguish (c), (d), and (e) from one another as separate and distinct claims about the being than-which-a-greater-cannot-be-thought. But it is not only in Chapter V that Anselm makes this distinction. This distinction is made and maintained throughout the entire *Reply*, and the *Reply* is a ten chapter commentary on *Proslogion* II and III in which Anselm attempts to explain and defend his reasoning in the *Proslogion*. Explicitly, the distinction that Anselm maintains is that the being than-which-a-greater-cannot-be-thought *exists*, that the being *cannot be thought not to exist*, and that the being *cannot not exist*. For Anselm (d) and (e) are clearly not alternative ways of asserting the same thing. For Anselm (d) and (e) are separate and different claims about the being than-which-a-greater-cannot-be-thought. Now if the transformation of Anselm's terminology in terms of necessity and logical possibility is legitimate and appropriate at all, it is surely Anselm's term "cannot not exist" (*non potest non esse*) and not his term "cannot be *thought* not to exist" (*non possit cogitari non esse*) that should be so transformed.

But even in this case the legitimacy of such a transformation is highly dubious. The problem is that Malcolm's and Charlesworth's transformations involve the notions of *logical* impossibility and *logical* necessity and it is not at all clear from the *Proslogion* or the *Reply* that Anselm means logically impossible by his term "*non posse non*". Anselm indicates in *Reply* VIII that the being that cannot not exist is the being that has neither a beginning nor end, in *Proslogion* XIII that the being that cannot not exist is limitless and eternal, and in *Proslogion* XIX that the being that cannot not exist is not in place or time. And, despite the fact that Malcolm argues that these attributes involve logically necessary existence, Anselm does not give us any reason to think that he regards these attributes as involving logically necessary existence. Rather, if Anselm's claims indicate anything, they indicate that to say that the being cannot not exist is to say that it has nether beginning nor end, that it is limitless and eternal, and that it is not in place or time.

Consequently even in Anselm's claim (e) there is no reason to suppose that he is asserting logically necessary existence of the being than-which-a-greater-cannot-be-thought, and it is a fiction to maintain the view that the transformation of Anselm's term "cannot be thought not to exist" into either "nonexistence is logically impossible" or "necessarily exists" represents the meaning of what Anselm intended to express in *Proslogion* III. Furthermore, it follows that even if *Proslogion* III contains an unintentional but logically complete and independent argument whose conclusion is (d), it does not contain a logically complete and independent argument whose conclusion is (G2). If there is a logically complete and independent argument in *Proslogion* III, all that it can possibly establish is (d) and (d) implies neither (c) nor (e). If *Proslogion* III establishes anything by itself then all that it establishes is that the being than-which-a-greater-cannot-be-thought cannot be thought not to exist.

But now, is there a logically complete and independent argument at all in *Proslogion* III? Is even claim (d) deducible from what would have to be the premises of *Proslogion* III if it contains a logically complete and independent argument? We have seen that Malcolm and Charlesworth read the second sentence of *Proslogion* III as

(i)   a being that cannot be thought not to exist is greater than a being that can be thought not to exist

and we have seen that their transformation of this premise to deduce (G2) is not a fathful representation of Anselm's intentions and, hence, that (G2) could not be deduced from it while representing that deduction as Anselm's argument. But not only do Malcolm's and

Charlesworth's transformations misrepresent Anselm's reasoning, it is not at all clear that their reading of Anselm's second sentence in *Proslogion* III accurately represents Anselm's reasoning and this is because it is not at all clear how Malcolm and Charlesworth would have us understand (i). If Malcolm and Charlesworth would have us understand (i) to mean

>   (ia) For any x, if x cannot be thought not to exist then x is greater than what can be thought not to exist

then even if (d) is deducible from Malcolm's and Charlesworth's premise (ia) that deduction could not be represented as Anselm's argument because Anselm does not assert (ia) in *Proslogion* III. What Anselm says is:

> For something can be thought to exist that cannot be thought not to exist, and this is greater than that which can be thought not to exist.[22]

Now Anselm certainly says that something is greater than what can be thought not to exist, but he does *not* say that *if* something cannot be thought not to exist then it is greater than what can be thought not to exist. Rather, what Anselm says is that something can be thought to exist that cannot be thought not to exist, and it is this which is greater than what can be thought not to exist. Consequently, if Malcolm and Charlesworth would have us understand (i) to mean (ia) then the argument which they identify cannot be attributed to Anselm.

If *Proslogion* III is to be interpreted as containing an unintentional but logically complete and independent argument whose conclusion is (d), then the premises of that argument must be

>   (ii) Something, x, can be thought to exist and cannot be thought not to exist,

and

>   (iii) x is greater than what can be thought not to exist.

But perhaps Malcolm and Charlesworth would have us understand their premise (i) to mean

>   (ib) Something, x, cannot be thought not to exist and x is greater than what can be thought not to exist.

---

[22] Anselm, p. 119.

Now it would appear that (ib) is substantially the same as the conjunction of Anselm's (ii) and (iii) except that (ib) does not contain the further claim of (ii) that x can be thought to exist. This difference could be easily remedied. But if Malcolm and Charlesworth would have us understand (i) to mean (ib) and if (ib) is substantially the same claim as the conjunction of Anselm's (ii) and (iii) then while it is possible to deduce (d) from (ib) because it is possible to deduce (d) from Anselm's (ii) alone, that deduction is so trivial that there is no apparent reason to treat it either as an argument which Anselm is offering or an argument to which Anselm is committed even though he did not intend to offer one.

This becomes apparent if we keep in mind that the primary assumption upon which all of Anselm's reasoning rests is the assumption that something-than-which-a-greater-cannot-be-thought can be thought to exist. This assumption is asserted in *Proslogion* II and in almost every chapter of the *Reply*. In fact in some chapters of the *Reply* it is asserted repeatedly. It is an assumption which is absolutely necessary to the entire structure of Anselm's reasoning, and if we do not at least provisionally accept that assumption, then Anselm's reasoning does not even get under way. In addition, it must be realized that Anselm explicitly states in *Reply* IV that something-than-which-a-greater-cannot-be-thought is unique as that which cannot be thought not to exist. Because of these facts it should be apparent that for Anselm the term "something-than-which-a-greater-cannot-be-thought" is the only term which can be substituted for x in (ii) and (iii) which yield true statements. So, for Anselm (ii) is equivalent to

(ii′) Something-than-which-a-greater-cannot-be-thought can be thought to exist and cannot be thought not to exist

and (iii) is equivalent to

(iii′) Something-than-which-a-greater-cannot-be-thought is greater than what can be thought not to exist.

Now if (ib) is substantially the same as the conjunction of Anselm's (ii) and (iii) then (ib) is equivalent to

(ib′) Something-than-which-a-greater-cannot-be-thought cannot be thought not to exist and is greater than what can be thought not to exist.

So, if (ib) is substantially the same as the conjunction of Anselm's (ii) and (iii) then while it is possible to deduce (d) from (ib′) and (ii′) and, hence, from (i) and (ii), that deduction is so trivial that there is no reason to treat it as an argument to which Anselm is committed. Since there is no evidence that Anselm thought of himself as offering two different proofs, there would seem to be no reason to treat the *possible* deduction of (d) from (ii) as an argument presented by Anselm in *Proslogion* III, and since the deduction of (d) from (ii) is so trivial there would seem to be no reason to treat the *possible* deduction of (d) from (ii) as an argument unnoticed by Anselm, but nevertheless, present in *Proslogion* III. On the other hand, if (ib) is *not* substantially the same as the conjunction of Anselm's (ii) and (iii) then even if (d) is deducible from (ib) in a way that is not trivial that deduction does not represent an argument to which Anselm is committed since Anselm would not then be committed to (ib). In either case, then, it appears that *Proslogion* III does not contain a logically complete and independent argument for even assertion (d), at least not any argument that can be attributed to Anselm or one to which he is committed as accepting as his own.

The result of examining *Proslogion* III and the *Reply* is that we do not find what we would expect to find from being told by the proponents of the new interpretation that *Proslogion* III contains a logically complete and independent argument whose conclusion is (G2). Anselm does not conclude his reasoning in *Proslogion* III with the proposition (G2) but with the more complex proposition (c)-(d)-(e). Even when we allow the transformation of Anselm's terminology, his concluding proposition is still the complex proposition (c)-(d)-(e), and his sentences that would have to be the premises of this argument, if it is an argument, are not strong enough to support that conclusion. In view of the fact that (G2) does not imply (e) and that there is no more reason to suppose that Anselm was attempting to provide an argument for (G2) than there is to suppose he was attempting to provide an argument for (e), it follows, as the *Reply* indicates, that *Proslogion* III was not intended by Anselm to be a logically complete and independent argument.

Even if we allow the possibility that despite Anselm's intentions the sentences of *Proslogion* III constitute a logically complete and independent argument for (G2) though not for (e), it turns out that (G2) is not deducible from *Proslogion* III unless (d) is deducible and we allow the transformation of Anselm's terminology. But, then, such an argument cannot be attributed to Anselm because the transformation of Anselm's terminology is not only unjustified, but it is both inconsistent with his other intentions as they are reflected in other assertions of the *Proslogion* and inconsistent with his own practice in the *Reply*. Even if we abandon the transformations, (d) is not deducible in such a way that the deduction could be seriously represented as Anselm's argument because what would have to count as the premises of *Proslogion* III would make the deduction of (d) a trivial deduction.

It follows, then, that Anselm did not provide, either intentionally or unintentionally, a logically complete and independent argument in *Proslogion* III; and, hence, the proponents of the new interpretation are incorrect in treating *Proslogion* III as a logically complete and independent argument. The new interpretation is, in this respect, an inadequate interpretation of Anselm's existential reasoning. But not only is it the case that the new interpretation is inadequate, it is also the case that this inadequacy of the new interpretation substantiates the third or alternative interpretation as well as Anselm's claim in *Reply* X about the relationship that obtains between *Proslogion* II and *Proslogion* III. Both the third or alternative interpretation and *Reply* X represent the claim that *Proslogion* II and *Proslogion* III must be taken together, and that together they constitute the basis for a series of existential deductions about the being than-which-a-greater-cannot-be-thought.

Now a rejection of the third or alternative interpretation or a rejection of *Reply* X would constitute the denial that *Proslogion* II and *Proslogion* III must be taken together in this way, and, unless it were maintained and established that *Proslogion* II and *Proslogion* III are independent of one another even though neither one contains a logically complete argument, such a denial could only be justified on the grounds that at least one of these two Chapters actually contains a logically complete and independent argument. Accordingly, the inadequacy of the new interpretation, that *Proslogion* III does not contain a logically complete and independent argument, substantiates the third or alternative interpretation and *Reply* X by showing that *Proslogion* III does not provide grounds for denying the claim about the relationship between *Proslogion* II and *Proslogion* III, and, hence, *Proslogion* III does not provide grounds for rejecting the third or alternative interpretation and *Reply* X as an accurate interpretation of Anselm's existential reasoning.

But while the inadequacy of the new interpretation substantiates *Reply* X and the third or alternative interpretation, it does not by itself show that in order to be interpreted accurately *Proslogion* II and *Proslogion* III must be interpreted in the way that is represented by *Reply* X and the third or alternative interpretation, because there still remain other possible grounds for rejecting this way of interpreting *Proslogion* II and *Proslogion* III. First, there is the possibility that *Proslogion* II does in fact contain a logically complete and independent argument, and, so, there is the possibility that *Proslogion* II provides grounds for rejecting *Reply* X and the third or alternative interpretation. Second, there is the possibility that *Proslogion* II and *Proslogion* III are in fact independent of one another even though neither of these two Chapters contains a logically complete argument and, so, there is the possibility that *Proslogion* II and *Proslogion* III considered together provide grounds for rejecting *Reply* X and the third or alternative interpretation. If it could be shown that *Proslogion* II cannot be treated as a logically complete and independent argument which can be reasonably attributed to Anselm, then it would also be shown that *Proslogion* II provides no grounds for rejecting *Reply* X and the third or alternative interpretation. It would follow from this either that in order to be interpreted accurately *Proslogion* II and *Proslogion* III must be interpreted in the way that is represented by *Reply* X and the third or alternative interpretation or else that *Proslogion* II and *Proslogion* III are in fact independent of one another even though neither one of these two Chapters contains a logically complete argument. The next task, then, is to compare the current interpretations with *Proslogion* II and the *Reply* in order to show that *Proslogion* II cannot be interpreted as containing a logically complete and independent argument which can be reasonably attributed to Anselm.

The Alleged Proslogion II Argument

According to the proponents of both of the current interpretations, *Proslogion* II contains a logically complete and independent argument for the existence of God. Unlike the way in which the proponents of the new interpretation hedge on the question of whether *Proslogion* III was intended by Anselm to represent a logically complete and independent argument, neither the proponents of the traditional interpretation nor the proponents of the new interpretation even question the doctrine that *Proslogion* II was intended by Anselm to represent a logically complete and independent argument. The proponents of the current interpretations simply assume that this doctrine represents Anselm's intentions in *Proslogion* II, and then they proceed to construct a logically complete and independent argument from the assertions of *Proslogion* II. Since the proponents of the current interpretations establish that such an argument can be constructed, it would seem that it has been established that Anselm did, in fact, provide such an argument whether or not he intended to do so. But from the fact that the proponents of the current interpretations are able to construct a logically complete and independent argument from the assertions of *Proslogion* II, it does not follow, it is not thereby established, that Anselm did in fact provide such an argument.

It is one thing to construct such an argument and thereby establish that such an argument *can* be constructed and quite a different thing altogether to establish that Anselm is committed to that argument. The proponents of the current interpretations construct such an argument, but they never even attempt to establish that the argument which they identify is an argument to which Anselm is committed, and, hence, they never establish that *Proslogion* II does in fact contain a logically complete and independent argument. In order to establish that *Proslogion* II contains a logically complete and independent argument, the proponents of the current interpretations would have to establish that Anselm's assertions in *Proslogion* II and the *Reply* commit him to the argument which they identify. On the other hand, if it were shown that Anselm's assertions in *Proslogion* II and the *Reply* do not commit him to the argument which the proponents of the current interpretations identify, then there would be no reason for thinking that *Proslogion* II contains a logically complete and independent argument.

The proponents of the current interpretations maintain that *Proslogion* II contains a logically complete and independent argument whose conclusion is (c), that the being than-which-a-greater-cannot-be-thought exists in reality. Perhaps the most remarkable feature of the current interpretations is that none of the proponents of these interpretations, neither critics nor defenders, ever disagree about what the argument is which *Proslogion* II allegedly contains. There are disputes about whether the argument is valid or invalid, about whether the argument involves this mistake or that mistake, about whether the argument should be altered in this way or that way in order to salvage it, and so on; but except for differences in presentation or formulation, *all* the proponents of the current interpretations identify essentially the same argument as *the* argument of *Proslogion* II.

There are only three types of cases which could possibly be considered as an exception to this generalization, and these are cases in which the argument formulated does not correspond to the argument identified by the proponents of the current interpretations as *the Proslogion* II argument. But in cases like these the commentator cannot properly be said to be interpreting *Proslogion* II. First, there is the type of case in which the argument formulated is an alteration of some previous formulation which in turn does correspond to the argument identified by the proponents of the current interpretations as *the Proslogion* II argument. Surely such an argument cannot be regarded as an interpretation of *Proslogion* II.

Second, there is the type of case in which the commentator hedges on the question of whether or not the argument he formulates is an argument in *Proslogion* II. For example, in a chapter entitled "St. Anselm's Four Ontological Arguments for God's Existence," Professor Nakhnikian introduces his four arguments by remarking that he "...shall examine four ontological arguments that are strongly suggested, if not explicitly found, in St. Anselm."[23] This kind of qualification certainly forestalls the objection that the argument presented is not an argument provided by Anselm, but it also prohibits any claim to be interpreting *Proslogion* II.

Finally, there is the type of case in which the commentator confuses Anselm's reasoning with the argument of some other philosopher. Leibnitz, for example, purports to offer a criticism of Anselm in which the argument he formulates for criticism does not correspond to the argument identified by the proponents of the current interpretations as *the Proslogion* II argument. But the argument which Leibnitz[24] formulates for criticism cannot be regarded as an interpretation of *Proslogion* II because that argument is simply a bad formulation of the argument which Descartes gives in

---

[23] George Nakhnikian, *An Introduction to Philosophy* (New York: Alfred A. Knopf, Inc., 1967), p. 226.

[24] Gottfried Wilhelm Leibnitz, *Philosophical Papers and Letters*, trans. and ed. Leroy E. Loemker (Chicago: The University of Chicago Press, 1956), V. II, pp. 634-636.

Meditation V, and surely Descartes' argument cannot be reasonably regarded as an interpretation of *Proslogion* II. Accordingly, cases of these types cannot properly be regarded as exceptions to the general claim that all the proponents of the current interpretations of *Proslogion* II identify essentially the same argument as *the* argument of *Proslogion* II, because cases of these types cannot be reasonably represented as interpretations of *Proslogion* II at all.

When the differences of presentation or formulation are disregarded, the various versions of the argument which all the proponents of the current interpretations identify as *the* argument of *Proslogion* II always have two common features. First, the conclusion of the argument is always identified as assertion (c). Second, the major premise of the argument is always identified as the assertion or some slight variation of the assertion that

(h) Existence in reality is greater than existence in the mind alone.

Now, if Anselm is indeed committed to the argument which the proponents of the current interpretations identify, then he is committed to both assertion (c) and assertion (h). If Anselm is not committed to one of these assertions, then it follows that he is not committed to the argument identified by the proponents of the current interpretations or, in fact, to any argument which relies on that assertion.

One way to be committed to an assertion is to make that assertion. Obviously Anselm is committed to (c) in this way. He explicitly asserts (c) as the conclusion of the reasoning of *Proslogion* II, but this does not imply that (c) is the conclusion of some logically complete and independent piece of reasoning and it certainly does not imply that (c) is the conclusion of a piece of reasoning which requires that Anselm be committed to assertion (h) as one of its premises. But while Anselm is committed to assertion (c) by virtue of the fact that he asserts (c), he is most certainly not committed to assertion (h) in this way. The proposition that existence in reality is greater than existence in the mind alone does not even occur in *Proslogion* II as one of Anselm's assertions. What Anselm says in the reasoning of *Proslogion* II is

> And surely that-than-which-a-greater-cannot-be-thought cannot exist in the mind alone. For *if it exists solely in the mind even, it can be*

thought to exist in reality also, which is greater [italics mine]. If then that-than-which-a-greater-cannot-be-thought exists in the mind alone, this same that-than-which-a-greater-*cannot*-be-thought is that-than-which-a-greater-*can*-be-thought. But this is obviously impossible. Therefore there is absolutely no doubt that something-than-which-a-greater-cannot-be-thought exists both in the mind and in reality.[25]

Now, the italicized second sentence is the only proposition in the reasoning of *Proslogion* II which even approximates assertion (h), and it is the only one which could possibly provide grounds for the claim by the proponents of the current interpretations that (h) is one of Anselm's premises in this alleged argument. But the second sentence is manifestly not assertion (h), nor is it even similar enough to assertion (h) to justify the claim that Anselm is committed to (h) by virtue of the fact that he asserts (h) in *Proslogion* II. Assertion (h) simply does not occur in *Proslogion* II. Not only is it the case that (h) does not occur in *Proslogion* II, it is also the case that (h) does not occur anywhere in the *Proslogion* or the *Reply*. Anselm simply does not assert that existence in reality is greater than existence in the mind alone. The only place in which assertion (h) occurs is in Gaunilo's *Reply in Behalf of the Fool* (specifically, the first Chapter), and while Anselm does not explicitly repudiate the accuracy of Gaunilo's use of (h), Anselm does make it clear in *Reply* II that the proposition he intends to assert is the second sentence of the reasoning of *Proslogion* II. In *Reply* II Anselm responds to Gaunilo's objections by restating the reasoning of *Proslogion* II, and he gives precisely the same formulation to his assertion in *Reply* II that he does to his assertion of the second sentence of the reasoning of *Proslogion* II. This fact is significant because Anselm's restatement of his reasoning as it occurs in *Reply* II is not in all respects precisely the same as the original statement of his reasoning as it occurs in *Proslogion* II. In short, Anselm is not committed to assertion (h) by virtue of the fact that he asserts (h) because he does not assert (h).

But there are ways of being committed to an assertion other than by making that assertion. One can be committed to an assertion by virtue of the fact that a proposition he utters implies that assertion. Perhaps, then, Anselm is committed to assertion (h) on the grounds that the second sentence of the reasoning of *Proslogion* II implies

---

[25] Anselm, p. 117.

assertion (h). However, it should be obvious that Anselm's second sentence does not imply (h). Anselm can quite consistently deny that what exists in reality is greater than what exists in the mind alone and still claim that if the being than-which-a-greater-cannot-be-thought exists solely in the mind even, it can be thought to exist in reality also, which is greater. Accordingly, Anselm is not committed to assertion (h) on the grounds that Anselm's second sentence implies (h).

So far then, Anselm is not committed to assertion (h) either by making the assertion or by implication. But there is still one more way to be committed to an assertion. One can be committed to an assertion by virtue of the fact that the assertion is required to make his reasoning formally valid. Perhaps, then, Anselm is committed to assertion (h) by virtue of the fact that (h) is required to make *Proslogion* II formally valid. However, there are three difficulties with this suggestion. First, even if it is true that assertion (h) renders *Proslogion* II formally valid, it does not follow that (h) is the only such proposition, and, hence, it does not follow that assertion (h) itself is *required* to make *Proslogion* II formally valid. In order to show that assertion (h) is required it would be necessary to establish not only that assertion (h) does render *Proslogion* II formally valid but also that no other proposition would. Second, even if it were true that assertion (h) is required to make *Proslogion* II formally valid, it does not follow that Anselm is committed to assertion (h) unless it is also true that Anselm intended that *Proslogion* II, by itself, be formally valid. Since Anselm's claims in the *Preface* and *Reply* X make it quite plain that he did not intend that *Proslogion* II, by itself, be formally valid, then Anselm is not committed to assertion (h), or to any other assertion for that matter, on the grounds that the assertion renders *Proslogion* II formally valid. Third, even if Anselm were committed to assertion (h) on the grounds that (h) is required to make *Proslogion* II formally valid, it would not follow that *Proslogion* II contains a logically complete argument as the proponents of the current interpretations claim. In fact, just the opposite would follow, for to hold the view that assertion (h) is required to make *Proslogion* II formally valid is to hold the view that *Proslogion* II is not logically complete without assertion (h). In short, Anselm is not committed to assertion (h) in this way of being committed to an assertion and, even if he were in fact so committed, it would follow that *Proslogion* II does not contain a logically complete argument.

The result of comparing the current interpretations with *Proslogion* II and the *Reply* is that Anselm is *not* committed to assertion (h), and, hence, he is *not* committed to the argument identified by the proponents of the current interpretations. The argument identified by the proponents of the current interpretations is no doubt an interesting philosophical argument, and it certainly provides grounds for interesting philosophical discussion, but it is not an argument that can be attributed to Anselm. It cannot be claimed that the argument is Anselm's argument. In view of Anselm's avowed intention of providing *one* proof from which can be deduced whatever must be believed about the Divine Being, there is no reason to think that *Proslogion* II does contain a logically complete argument. In fact a careful reading of the reasoning of *Proslogion* II should make it obvious that the reasoning as it stands is not logically complete. Assertion (c) simply does not follow from Anselm's other assertions as they are stated. Only if it is mistakenly assumed that Anselm intended to provide a logically complete argument in *Proslogion* II, can a case be made for the view that *Proslogion* II does contain such an argument and then only if some additional premise is added to make the reasoning logically complete. As it stands, the reasoning of *Proslogion* II is not logically complete, and this fact is quite consistent with Anselm's intentions as they are expressed in the *Preface* and *Reply* X.

It turns out that Anselm did not provide a logically complete and independent argument in *Proslogion* II and that the proponents of the current interpretations are incorrect in treating *Proslogion* II as a logically complete and independent argument. The current interpretations are, in this respect, inadequate interpretations of Anselm's existential reasoning. Furthermore, this inadequacy of the current interpretations, that *Proslogion* II does not contain a logically complete and independent argument, substantiates the third or alternative interpretation and *Reply* X by showing that *Proslogion* II does not provide grounds for denying the claim that *Proslogion* II and *Proslogion* III must be taken together in the specified way; and, hence, *Proslogion* II does not provide grounds for rejecting the third or alternative interpretation and *Reply* X as an accurate interpretation of Anselm's existential reasoning.

Since the other possible interpretations have been eliminated, it follows, then, either that in order to be interpreted accurately *Proslogion* II and *Proslogion* III must be interpreted in the way that is represented by *Reply* X and the third or alternative interpretation or else that *Proslogion* II and *Proslogion* III are in fact independent of one another even though neither one of these two Chapters contains a logically complete argument. But except for the fact that it is a formal possibility, this latter view (that *Proslogion* II and *Proslogion* III are in fact independent of one another even though neither of these two Chapters contains a logically complete argument) does not provide grounds for rejecting *Reply* X and the third or alternative interpretation because there are no apparent grounds at all for holding this view. To adopt this view is to assume that Anselm did not provide a set of propositions from which *any* of his assertions (c), (d), or (e) are deducible, and this is to assume that Anselm did not provide any argument at all. Surely, then, to adopt such a view is to completely abandon the *Proslogion* as a philosophical work, and such an approach is clearly inconsistent with the obvious philosophical characteristics of Anselm's reasoning. It follows, then, that in order to be interpreted accurately, *Proslogion* II and *Proslogion* III must be interpreted in the way that is represented by *Reply* X and the third or alternative interpetation.

A Positive Justification For
The Third or Alternative Interpretation

But while the third or alternative interpretation turns out to be the winner among competing interpretations, it has so far won only by default. The third or alternative interpretation has been established to be the accurate interpretation of Anselm's existential reasoning, but it has only been established negatively on the grounds that the inadequacy of the current interpretations and the inadequacy of the new interpretation show that neither *Proslogion* II nor *Proslogion* III provides grounds for rejecting the third or alternative interpretation. The ideal, however, would be to show in a positive way that *Proslogion* II and *Proslogion* III provide grounds for accepting the third or alternative interpretation. It turns out that there is such a positive justification because not only is it the case that these inadequacies substantiate in a negative way the third or alternative interpretation, it is also the case that these inadequacies suggest in a positive way the third or alternative interpretation.

Both the inadequacy of the new interpretation and the inadequacy of the current interpretations suggest the third or alternative interpretation and these inadequacies indicate how it is that *Proslogion* II and *Proslogion* III provide grounds for accepting the third or alternative interpretation. Although the argument which shows that the inadequacy of the new interpretation suggests the third or alternative interpretation is similar and parallel to the argument which shows that the inadequacy of the current interpretations suggests the third or alternative interpretation, it is necessary to present these arguments separately because, unlike the proponents of the new interpretation, the proponents of the traditional interpretation are not committed to the view that *Proslogion* III contains a logically complete and independent argument. Accordingly, the next task is first to show that the inadequacy of the *new* interpretation suggests the third or alternative interpretation and, second, to show that the inadequacy of the *current* interpretations suggests the third or alternative interpretation.

The new interpretation is inadequate because it incorrectly treats *Proslogion* III as a logically complete and independent argument. But how does this inadequacy of the new interpretation suggest the third or alternative interpretation, the interpretation implied by *Reply* X, beyond the fact that the third or alternative interpretation does not treat *Proslogion* III as a logically complete and independent argument? How does this inadequacy of the new interpretation suggest that *Proslogion* II and *Proslogion* III have to be taken together and that together they constitute the basis for a series of existential deductions about the being than-which-a-greater-cannot-be-thought?

In view of the fact that the traditional interpretation does not treat *Proslogion* III as a logically complete and independent argument, it might be supposed that what this inadequacy of the new interpretation actually suggests is the traditional interpretation. It might be supposed that this inadequacy of the new interpretation simply reduces the new interpretation to nothing more than the traditional interpretation. Accordingly, it might be supposed that the traditional interpretation is the sole alternative to the new interpretation and that the new interpretation enjoys exactly the same advantages and suffers from exactly the same defects as the traditional interpretation. But this assumes that the only difference between the current interpretations is that the new interpretation treats *Proslogion* III as a logically complete and independent argument while the traditional interpretation does not.

The fact is that the proponents of the new interpretation make *two* claims about *Proslogion* III which distinguish the new interpretation from the traditional interpretation. The proponents of the new interpretation hold both that *Proslogion* III is significant in Anselm's existential reasoning *and* that the significance of *Proslogion* III is that it contains a logically complete and independent argument. Even though *Proslogion* III does not contain a logically complete and independent argument as the proponents of the new interpretation claim, there still remains a difference between the current interpretations in that the new interpretation treats *Proslogion* III as significant in Anselm's existential reasoning while the traditional interpretation does not. Because of this difference between the current interpretations, the inadequacy of the new interpretation that *Proslogion* III does not contain a logically complete and independent argument does not reduce the new interpretation to the traditional interpretation. Because the new interpretation treats *Proslogion* III as significant in Anselm's existential reasoning and the traditional interpretation does not, the inadequacy of the new interpretation does not suggest the traditional interpretation.

In view of the fact that there is no apparent reason for rejecting the claim that *Proslogion* III is significant in Anselm's existential reasoning, what the inadequacy of the new interpretation suggests is that some explanation must be given of the significance of *Proslogion* III other than that it contains a logically complete and independent argument. In fact the very mistakes which the proponents of the new interpretation make in treating *Proslogion* III as a logically complete and independent argument suggest both that *Proslogion* III is significant in Anselm's existential reasoning and what that significance is. The mistakes which the proponents of the new interpretation make suggest the claim of the third or alternative interpretation, the claim which Anselm makes in *Reply* X, that *Proslogion* II and III have to be taken together and that together they constitute the basis for a series of existential deductions about the being than-which-a-greater-cannot-be-thought. Accordingly, it is necessary to re-examine the new interpretation and *Proslogion* III in order to see how it is that the mistakes made by the proponents of the new interpretation suggest the third or alternative interpretation and the claim made by Anselm in *Reply* X about the relationship between *Proslogion* II and III.

As we have already seen, the proponents of the new interpretation identify (d) as the conclusion of *Proslogion* III and they transform Anselm's phrase "cannot be thought not to exist" into either "necessarily exists" or "nonexistence is logically impossible" such that (d) is transformable into (G2) and the alleged premises are transformable into propositions from which (G2) is deducible. Both the identification of the conclusion and the transformations are mistakes, but it seems that the former mistake is the more fundamental one because if the actual conclusion of the reasoning of *Proslogion* III had been properly identified, then, while it is possible, it is highly unlikely that the mistake of transforming Anselm's phrases would have been made. If it had been recognized by the proponents of the new interpretation that the actual conclusion of the reasoning of *Proslogion* III is the complex proposition (c)-(d)-(e), then it would have been apparent that Anselm clearly distinguishes between what cannot not exist and what cannot be *thought* not to exist. With such a clear distinction apparent, it would have been obvious that if the transformation in terms of logical possibility is at all warranted for any of Anselm's phrases, then it is the phrase "cannot not exist" that could be so transformed and not the phrase "cannot be *thought* not to exist." It is unlikely, then, that any transformations would have been made, since it would be (e), not (d), that could be transformed into (G2) and since the alleged premises would not be transformable into propositions from which (G2) could be deduced because the alleged premises contain the phrase "cannot be *thought* not to exist" and not the phrase "cannot not exist." It is the mistake of not properly identifying the conclusion of the reasoning of *Proslogion* III which leads the proponents of the new interpretation into the mistake of transforming Anselm's phrases in terms of logical possibility. Accordingly, it is the mistake of incorrectly identifying the conclusion of the reasoning of *Proslogion* III which is the fundamental mistake of the proponents of the new interpretation, and it is primarily, though not solely, this mistake which suggests the third or alternative interpretation.

When it is recognized that the conclusion of the reasoning of *Proslogion* III is the complex proposition (c)-(d)-(e), it becomes obvious that the reasoning of *Proslogion* III is not by itself sufficient to support the conclusion. This fact suggests two possibilities. Either Anselm asserted a proposition in *Proslogion* III for which he provided no justification or Anselm asserted a proposition in *Proslogion* III the justification of which he had no intention of providing in *Proslogion* III alone. But since there is no apparent reason to think that Anselm asserted a proposition in *Proslogion* III for which he provided no justification, the mistake made by the proponents of the new interpretation of incorrectly identifying the conclusion of the reasoning of *Proslogion* III suggests that the significance of *Proslogion* III in Anselm's existential reasoning is that *Proslogion* II and *Proslogion* III must be taken together and that together they support the conclusion (c)-(d)-(e).

At this point the objection might be raised that the preceding argument rests on two assumptions that have not been established: the assumption that *Proslogion* III is significant in Anselm's existential reasoning and the assumption that it is false that Anselm asserted a proposition in *Proslogion* III for which he provided no justification. There are two responses to this objection. First, there is no body of doctrine which has been defended nor any argument or set of arguments which these assumptions contradict. The proponents of the traditional interpretation simply ignore *Proslogion* III. If they can be said to have a doctrine at all about *Proslogion* III it is a doctrine of silence and it remains completely undefended. The very presence and character of the reasoning of *Proslogion* III, particularly in view of Anselm's claims in the *Preface* and *Reply* X, places the burden of proof with respect to these assumptions on the proponents of the traditional interpretation. As for the proponents of the new interpretation the first assumption is one of their own and the second assumption perpetuates the first in face of the fact that their own account of the first assumption fails.

Second, while these assumptions cannot be established formally by showing they are conclusions of *a priori* arguments presented by Anselm, a careful examination of *Proslogion* III and its contextual relationship with *Proslogion* II shows that Anselm's actual procedure in *Proslogion* II and III is faithfully represented by both of these assumptions as well as the interpretation they suggest, namely, that *Proslogion* II and III must be taken together and that together they support the conclusion (c)-(d)-(e). Not only is it the case that both of these assumptions are consistent with and faithfully represented by Anselm's claims in *Reply* X about *Proslogion* II and III, it is also the case that both of these assumptions and Anselm's claims in *Reply* X about *Proslogion* II and III are consistent with and faithfully represented by Anselm's actual procedure in *Proslogion* II and III.

Anselm concludes the reasoning of *Proslogion* II by arguing that

> Therefore there is absolutely no doubt that something-than-which-a-greater-cannot-be-thought exists both in the mind and in reality.[26]

Immediately following this he presents the reasoning of *Proslogion* III by arguing

> And certainly this being so truly exists that it cannot be even thought not to exist. For something can be thought to exist that cannot be thought not to exist, and this is greater than that which can be thought not to exist. Hence, if that-than-which-a-greater-cannot-be-thought can be thought not to exist, then that-than-which-a-greater-cannot-be-thought is not the same as that-than-which-a-greater-cannot-be-thought, which is absurd. Something-than-which-a-greater-cannot-be-thought exists so truly then, that it cannot be even thought not to exist.[27]

At this point what should be noticed about Anselm's actual procedure is that the reasoning of *Proslogion* III both begins and ends with the conclusion (c)-(d)-(e). The first and superficial response to this fact might be to suggest that it simply represents the procedure of first stating what *is to be* proved in *Proslogion* III and then restating what *has been* proved in *Proslogion* III. The context, however, suggests a slightly different procedure. The last occurrence of the conclusion most certainly has the force of the claim that (c)-(d)-(e) has been established by what precedes it. Anselm's procedure manifestly involves this claim. But the last occurrence of the conclusion does not have the force of the claim that (c)-(d)-(e) is deducible *solely* from the assertions of *Proslogion* III. It is an indisputable and significant fact that in Anselm's actual procedure the assertions of *Proslogion* II as well as the assertions of *Proslogion* III precede the last occurrence of the conclusion, and since *Proslogion* III alone is not even superficially sufficient to support (c)-(d)-(e), what is significant about this fact is that it suggests that (c)-(d)-(e) was not intended by Anselm to be supported solely by the assertions of *Proslogion* III.

The fact that the last occurrence of the conclusion has the force of the claim that (c)-(d)-(e) is deducible from the assertions which preceded it, conjoined with both the fact that the assertions of *Proslogion* II as well as the assertions of *Proslogion* III precede the last occurrence of the conclusion and the fact that *Proslogion* III is

---

[26] *Ibid.*
[27] Anselm, p. 119.

not by itself sufficient to support (c)-(d)-(e) suggests that (c)-(d)-(e) was intended by Anselm to be deducible from the assertions of both *Proslogion* II and *Proslogion* III taken together. Accordingly, the force of the claim involved in the last occurrence of the conclusion is consistent with and is faithfully represented by both the assumption that *Proslogion* III is significant in Anselm's existential reasoning as well as the assumption that it is false that Anselm asserted a proposition in *Proslogion* III for which he provided no justification. The last occurrence of the conclusion indicates that *Proslogion* II and *Proslogion* III must be taken together and that together they support the conclusion (c)-(d)-(e).

The first occurrence of the conclusion indicates the same interpretation because the first occurrence of the conclusion cannot be represented in Anselm's procedure as serving the function of stating what is to be proved by the assertions of *Proslogion* III alone. The fact is obvious that the assertions which follow the first occurrence of the conclusion simply do not constitute a proof for (c)-(d)-(e). Accordingly, the first occurrence of the conclusion does not have the force of the claim that (c)-(d)-(e) is to be proved solely by the assertions which follow it. What, then, is the force of the claim involved in the first occurrence of the conclusion, and what do the assertions which follow the first occurrence of the conclusion constitute if not a proof? Notice first that in the last sentence of *Proslogion* II Anselm claims that (c) is deducible from the reasoning of *Proslogion* II. What immediately follows this claim is the assertion (c)-(d)-(e), which occurs in the very first sentence of *Proslogion* III. But why does Anselm assert (c)-(d)-(e) in the first sentence of *Proslogion* III? In view of the fact that he has just claimed that (c) is deducible from the reasoning of *Proslogion* II, why should Anselm assert (c) as well as (d) and (e) in the first sentence of *Proslogion* III unless he is claiming there that (d) and (e) have exactly the same logical status as (c), that is, the logical status of being deducible from the reasoning of *Proslogion* II? The contextual relationship of *Proslogion* II and *Proslogion* III indicates that the first occurrence of the conclusion in *Proslogion* III has the force of the claim that (c)-(d)-(e) is deducible from the assertions which precede it. What Anselm is saying in the first sentence of *Proslogion* III is that not only is it the case that (c) is deducible from the assertions which precede, but it is also the case that (d) and (e) are deducible from the assertions which precede. In support of the claim that (c), (d), and (e) are deducible from the reasoning of *Proslogion* II, Anselm gives directions for performing these deductions. The assertions following the first occurrence of the conclusion of *Proslogion* III constitute these directions, and, as we shall see later, these directions in *Proslogion* III indicate how the very compact reasoning of *Proslogion* II is to be unpacked or filled out in order to deduce (c)-(d)-(e). The first occurrence of the conclusion, then, also indicates that *Proslogion* II and *Proslogion* III must be taken together and that together they support the conclusion (c)-(d)-(e).

The result, then, of examining the contextual relationship between *Proslogion* II and *Proslogion* III indicates that Anselm's actual procedure in *Proslogion* II and III is consistent with and is faithfully represented by both the assumption that *Proslogion* III is significant in Anselm's existential reasoning and the assumption that it is false that Anselm asserted a proposition in *Proslogion* III for which he provided no justification. Such an examination shows that the mistake made by the proponents of the new interpretation of incorrectly identifying the conclusion of *Proslogion* III does in fact suggest that the significance of *Proslogion* III in Anselm's existential reasoning is that *Proslogion* II and III must be taken together and that together they support the conclusion (c)-(d)-(e). Not only is it the case that the inadequacy of the new interpretation substantiates the third or alternative interpretation, it is also the case that this inadequacy suggests the third or alternative interpretation by showing that *Proslogion* III provides positive grounds for accepting the third or alternative interpretation.

In a similar way the inadequacy of the current interpretations suggests the third or alternative interpretation. But how does the inadequacy of the current interpretations suggest the third or alternative interpretation, the interpretation implied by *Reply* X, beyond the fact that the third or alternative interpretation does not treat *Proslogion* II as a logically complete and independent argument? How does the inadequacy of the current interpretations suggest that *Proslogion* II and *Proslogion* III have to be taken together and that together they constitute the basis for a series of existential deductions about the being than-which-a-greater-cannot-be-thought? In view of the fact that half of the new interpretation and all of the traditional interpretation is represented by the claim that *Proslogion* II contains a logically complete and independent argument, it might be supposed that this inadequacy of the current interpretations suggests *only* that half of the new interpretation and all of the traditional interpretation must be rejected. But this approach assumes that the only claim involved in the current interpretations is the claim that *Proslogion* II contains a logically complete and independent argument.

The fact is that the proponents of the current interpretations make *two* claims about *Proslogion* II. The proponents of the current interpretations hold both that *Proslogion* II is significant in Anselm's existential reasoning and that the significance of *Proslogion* II is that it contains a logically complete and independent argument. Even though *Proslogion* II does not contain a logically complete and independent argument as the proponents of the current interpretations claim, there still remains the unrefuted residual claim that *Proslogion* II is significant in Anselm's existential reasoning. Because of this residual claim the inadequacy of the current interpretations does not suggest that half of the new interpretation and all of the traditional interpretation must be rejected *in toto*.

In view of the fact that there is no apparent reason for rejecting the claim that *Proslogion* II is significant in Anselm's existential reasoning, what the inadequacy of the current interpretations suggests is that some explanation must be given of the significance of *Proslogion* II other than that it contains a logically complete and independent argument. In fact, the very mistake which the proponents of the current interpretations make in treating *Proslogion* II as a logically complete and independent argument suggests both that *Proslogion* II is significant in Anselm's existential reasoning and what that significance is. The mistake which the proponents of the current interpretations make in treating *Proslogion* II as a logically complete and independent argument suggests the claim of the third or alternative interpretation that *Proslogion* II and *Proslogion* III have to be taken together and that together they constitute the basis for a series of existential deductions about the being than-which-a-greater-cannot-be-thought. Accordingly, it is necessary to re-examine the current interpretations and *Proslogion* II in order to see how it is that the mistake made by the proponents of the current interpretations suggests the third or alternative interpretation and the claim made by Anselm in *Reply* X about the relationship between *Proslogion* II and *Proslogion* III.

As we have already seen the primary mistake made by the proponents of the current interpretations is to identify assertion (h) as

Anselm's major premise. Though it is plausible enough to assume that Anselm is committed to assertion (h) on the grounds that (h) is required to make *Proslogion* II formally valid, it no longer remains plausible to hold, along with that assumption, that *Proslogion* II contains a logically complete and independent argument; and when it is recognized that Anselm is not committed to assertion (h) on any grounds, it becomes obvious that the reasoning of *Proslogion* II is not by itself sufficient to support the conclusion (c).

This fact suggests two possibilities. Either Anselm asserted a proposition in *Proslogion* II for which he provided no justification, or Anselm asserted a proposition in *Proslogion* II the justification of which he had no intention of providing in *Proslogion* II alone. Since there is no reason to suppose that Anselm asserted a proposition in *Proslogion* II for which he provided no justification, the mistake made by the proponents of the current interpretations of incorrectly assuming that Anselm is committed to assertion (h) suggests that the significance of *Proslogion* II in Anselm's existential reasoning is that *Proslogion* II and *Proslogion* III must be taken together and that together they support the conclusion (c).

While the preceding argument rests on the two assumptions that *Proslogion* II is significant in Anselm's existential reasoning and that it is false that Anselm asserted a proposition in *Proslogion* II for which he provided no justification, there can be no objection to these assumptions by the proponents of the current interpretations because the first assumption is one of their own and the second assumption perpetuates the first in the face of the fact that their own account of the first assumption fails. In fact a denial of these assumptions on any grounds would involve abandoning the view that the *Proslogion* is a philosophical work, and this is inconsistent with the obvious philosophical characteristics of the reasoning of *Proslogion* II and *Proslogion* III. Furthermore, a careful examination of *Proslogion* II and its contextual relationship with *Proslogion* III shows that Anselm's actual procedure in *Proslogion* II and III is faithfully represented by both of these assumptions and the interpretation they suggest, namely, that *Proslogion* II and III must be taken together and that together they support the conclusion (c). Not only is it the case that both of these assumptions are consistent with and faithfully represented by Anselm's claims in *Reply* X about *Proslogion* II and III, it is also the case that both of these assumptions and Anselm's claims in *Reply* X about *Proslogion* II and III are consistent with and faithfully represented by Anselm's actual procedure in *Proslogion* II and III.

It has already been observed that Anselm concludes the reasoning of *Proslogion* II by asserting (c). The traditional response to this fact has been to suppose that it represents the procedure of deducing (c) solely from the assertions of *Proslogion* II which precede it. However, the assertion of (c) and its contextual relationship with *Proslogion* III suggests a slightly different procedure. While the assertion of (c) in *Proslogion* II most certainly has the force of the claim that (c) is deducible from the assertions of *Proslogion* II which precede it, the assertion of (c) does *not* have the force of the claim that (c) is deducible *solely* from the assertions of *Proslogion* II which precede it; and since (c) is in fact *not* deducible solely from the assertions in *Proslogion* II which precede it, the indisputable and significant fact that in Anselm's actual procedure he also asserts (c) in the conclusion (c)-(d)-(e) of the reasoning of *Proslogion* III suggests that in his actual procedure the conclusion (c) was not intended by Anselm to be supported *solely* by the assertions of *Proslogion* II. What is suggested is that *Proslogion* II and *Proslogion* III were intended by Anselm to be taken together to support the conclusion (c). Furthermore, the contextual relationship of the two occurrences of the conclusion (c)-(d)-(e) in *Proslogion* III with *Proslogion* II further suggests an intended mutual dependence between *Proslogion* II and *Proslogion* III.

The first occurrence of the conclusion (c)-(d)-(e) in *Proslogion* III immediately follows the assertion of (c) in *Proslogion* II. This first occurrence of (c)-(d)-(e) has the force of the claim that (c), (d), and (e) have exactly the same logical status; and, since the assertion of (c) in *Proslogion* II has the force of the claim that (c) has the logical status of being deducible from the assertions of *Proslogion* II which precede it, this first assertion of (c)-(d)-(e) has the force of the claim that (c), (d), and (e) are deducible from the assertions of *Proslogion* II which precede it. But this assertion of (c)-(d)-(e) does not have the force of the claim that (c), (d), and (e) are deducible *solely* from the assertions of *Proslogion* II which precede it, and in Anselm's actual procedure he continues his reasoning in *Proslogion* III and concludes that reasoning by a final assertion of the conclusion (c)-(d)-(e). This last occurrence of the conclusion (c)-(d)-(e) also has the force of the claim that (c), (d), and (e) are deducible from the assertions which precede it, but in this case the assertions which precede the last occurrence of (c)-(d)-(e) are the assertions of both *Proslogion* II and *Proslogion* III. So, in view of the fact that the assertions of *Proslogion* II are not by themselves sufficient to support either (c), (d), or (e) and in view of the fact that the assertions of *Proslogion* III are not by themselves sufficient to support either (c), (d), or (e), both the first and the last occurrence of the conclusion (c)-(d)-(e) in *Proslogion* III suggest that in Anselm's actual procedure (c), (d), and (e) are intended by Anselm to be deducible from the assertions of both *Proslogion* II and *Proslogion* III taken together.

The result, then, of examining *Proslogion* II and its contextual relationship with *Proslogion* III shows that Anselm's actual procedure in *Proslogion* II and III is consistent with and is faithfully represented by both the assumption that *Proslogion* II is significant in Anselm's existential reasoning and the assumption that it is false that Anselm asserted a proposition in *Proslogion* II for which he provided no justification. Such an examination shows that the mistake made by the proponents of the current interpretations of incorrectly assuming that Anselm is committed to assertion (h) does in fact suggest that the significance of *Proslogion* II in Anselm's existential reasoning is that *Proslogion* II and III must be taken together and that together they support not only (c) but (d) and (e) as well. Not only is it the case that the inadequacy of the current interpretations substantiates the third or alternative interpretation, it is also the case that this inadequacy suggests the third or alternative interpretation by showing that *Proslogion* II provides positive grounds for accepting the third or alternative interpretation.

It turns out that in order to be interpreted accurately *Proslogion* II and *Proslogion* III must be interpreted in the way that is represented by *Reply* X and the third or alternative interpretation. Both the inadequacy of the current interpretations and the inadequacy of the new interpretation substantiate *Reply* X and the third or alternative interpretation in a negative way by showing that neither *Proslogion* II nor *Proslogion* III provides grounds for rejecting *Reply* X and the third or alternative interpretation, but these inadequacies also suggest *Reply* X and the third or alternative interpretation in a positive way by showing that both *Proslogion* II and *Proslogion* III provide grounds for accepting *Reply* X and the third or alternative interpretation. In order to be interpreted accurately, *Proslogion* II and *Proslogion* III must be taken together in such a way that they constitute the basis for a series of existential deductions about the being than-which-a-greater-cannot-be-thought.

Summary

The major portion of the prescribed task is now complete. It has been shown that an analysis of the internal structure of *Proslogion* II and *Proslogion* III suggests the third or alternative interpretation when that analysis is guided both by Anselm's subsequent commentary on these two Chapters in the *Reply* and by a comparison of the current interpretations with the reasoning of *Proslogion* II and *Proslogion* III. That analysis revealed that Anselm does not purport to establish the existence of God in either *Proslogion* II or *Proslogion* III, but rather, that he purports to establish there the existence and something about the existence of the being than-which-a-greater-cannot-be-thought. It was also revealed that just as the *Preface* and *Reply* X indicated neither *Proslogion* II nor *Proslogion* III contains a logically complete and independent argument which can be reasonably attributed to Anselm and that if we are to preserve the obvious philosophical characteristics of Anselm's reasoning then *Proslogion* II and *Proslogion* III must be taken together in the way prescribed by the *Preface*, *Reply* X, and Anselm's actual procedure in *Proslogion* II and III.

The task now remains to examine in greater detail *Proslogion* II, *Proslogion* III, and the *Reply* in order to identify as precisely as possible how it is that *Proslogion* II and *Proslogion* III taken together constitute the basis for a series of existential deductions about the being than-which-a-greater-cannot-be-thought.

CHAPTER THREE

ANSELM'S REASONING

The central problem of this discussion is to determine what is the reasoning in and the relationship between *Proslogion* II and *Proslogion* III. So far we have discovered both what the relationship *is* between these two Chapters and what reasoning is *not* represented in them. We have discovered that neither the traditional interpretation nor the new interpretation accurately represents either the reasoning in or the relationship between *Proslogion* II and *Proslogion* III, and we have discovered that the inadequacies of these interpretations suggest that the relationship between *Proslogion* II and *Proslogion* III is that these two Chapters must be taken together and that together they constitute the basis for a series of existential deductions about the being than-which-a-greater-cannot-be-thought. What we have not yet discovered is how it is that *Proslogion* II and III are to be so taken together or what *is* the reasoning in these two Chapters. Accordingly, my present chapter is devoted to the task of examining *Proslogion* II, *Proslogion* III, and the *Reply* in order to identify as precisely as possible Anselm's reasoning in *Proslogion* II and III.

The Relationship Between the Reply and the Proslogion

However, before we begin this examination, it is perhaps advisable at the outset to make a few observations about the significance of the *Reply* to Anselm's existential reasoning of *Proslogion* II and III. Even a cursory reading makes it plain that the *Reply* is intended to function *primarily* as a response by Anselm to Gaunilo's criticism of the *Proslogion*. There can be no dispute about the fact that the *Reply* is intended to serve this primary function. There can be no dispute about the fact that the *Reply* is an explicit defense of the *Proslogion*. But both Hartshorne and Charlesworth, the only two commentators I am aware of who have anything substantive to say about the *Reply*, give a misleading account of both what it is in the *Proslogion* that Anselm defends in the *Reply* and the procedure which Anselm employs in his defense of the *Proslogion*; hence, they give a misleading account of the significance of the *Reply* to the *Proslogion*. Both of these commentators treat *Proslogion* III as an argument intended to establish the claim that

> (G3) the being than-which-a-greater-cannot-be-thought necessarily exists

and they treat certain Chapters of the *Reply* (Hartshorne:[1] *Reply* I, V, and IX; and Charlesworth: *Reply* I [2] and V[3]) as versions of, but arguments in addition to, the alleged *Proslogion* III argument which are themselves intended to establish the claim (G3). According to this treatment of the *Reply*, Anselm is defending *Proslogion* III by defending the *claim* of *Proslogion* III where this defense consists in providing arguments which are versions of, but in addition to, the alleged *Proslogion* III argument and which are themselves intended to establish the *claim* of *Proslogion* III that (G3). This treatment of the *Reply* is misleading for two reasons.

First, Hartshorne and Charlesworth fail to see that *Proslogion* III does not contain, nor was it intended to contain, a logically complete and independent argument. The result of this failure is that, in attempting to account for the way in which the *Reply* is a defense of *Proslogion* III, Chapters I, V, and IX of the *Reply* are treated as versions of the alleged *Proslogion* III argument (where those alleged versions are treated as arguments intended to establish the *claim* of *Proslogion* III). But since *Proslogion* III does not contain and was not intended to contain a logically complete and independent argument, neither *Reply* I, V, nor IX can contain arguments which can be treated as versions of the alleged *Proslogion* III argument. So, if the *Reply* is, at least in part, a defense of *Proslogion* III and if *Reply* I, V, and IX do in fact contain arguments then it cannot be maintained that the *Reply* is a defense of *Proslogion* III by maintaining that these alleged arguments of the *Reply* are arguments or versions of an argument which Anselm has presented in *Proslogion* III. According to this treatment of the *Reply*, the only way that it can be maintained that the *Reply* is a defense of *Proslogion* III is by maintaining that

---

[1] Charles Hartshorne, *Anselm's Discovery* (La Salle, Ill.: Open Court, 1965), p. 15.
[2] Anselm, *St. Anselm's Proslogion with a Reply on Behalf of the Fool by Gaunilo and the Author's Reply to Gaunilo*, trans. with an introduction and philosophical commentary by M.J. Charlesworth (Oxford: Clarendon Press, 1965), pp. 91-92.
[3] *Ibid.*, pp. 95-96.

Reply I, V, and IX contain arguments intended to establish the *claim* of *Proslogion* III that the being than-which-a-greater-cannot-be-thought necessarily exists.

But this latter way of maintaining that the *Reply* is a defense of *Proslogion* III is inconsistent with the view that the *Reply is* a defense of *Proslogion* III because the second reason why this treatment of the *Reply* is misleading is that Anselm's *Proslogion* III claim is *not* the claim that the being than-which-a-greater-cannot-be-thought necessarily exists (remember that "necessarily exists" is rendered by these commentators in terms of logical necessity). Anselm's *Proslogion* III claim is the complex claim (c)-(d)-(e) (here keep in mind that there is no reason to think that Anselm intends to assert anything about logical necessity when (d) or (e) are asserted). In short, Hartshorne and Charlesworth fail to accurately identify Anselm's *Proslogion* III claim. The result of this failure is that in attempting to account for the way in which the *Reply* is a defense of *Proslogion* III, Chapters I, V, and IX of the *Reply* are treated as arguments intended to establish the *claim* of *Proslogion* III. But Chapters I, V, and IX of the *Reply* are also treated as arguments intended to establish the claim (G3). So, because the claim of *Proslogion* III is *not* the claim (G3), if the *Reply* is treated as a defense of *Proslogion* III then neither *Reply* I, V, nor IX can be treated as arguments intended to establish the claim (G3); and if either *Reply* I, V, or IX are treated as arguments intended to establish the claim (G3), then the *Reply cannot* be treated as a defense of *Proslogion* III.

Therefore, it cannot be maintained both that the *Reply* is a defense of *Proslogion* III and that *Reply* I, V, and IX contain arguments intended to establish the claim that the being than-which-a-greater-cannot-be-thought necessarily exists. Either the *Reply* is *not* a defense of *Proslogion* III or neither *Reply* I, V, nor IX contains arguments intended to establish the claim (G3). On the assumption that the *Reply* is, at least in part, a defense of *Proslogion* III, it follows that neither *Reply* I, V, nor IX can be treated as an argument intended to establish the claim (G3) and some other explanation of the *Reply* must be given in order to account for it as a defense of *Proslogion* III. On the assumption that *Reply* I, V, and IX contain arguments intended to establish the claim (G3), it follows that the *Reply cannot* be treated as a defense of *Proslogion* III and some explanation must be given of the relationship between the *Reply* and

Proslogion III other than that the *Reply* is a defense of *Proslogion* III. But which assumption are we to make and which explanation is to be given?

Even a cursory reading makes it plain that the *Reply* is, at least in part and in some way, a defense of *Proslogion* III. It follows, then, that neither *Reply* I, V, nor IX can be treated as an argument intended to establish the claim (G3) and that some other explanation of the *Reply* must be given in order to account for it as a defense of *Proslogion* III. But not only is it the case that *Reply* I, V, and IX cannot be *treated* as arguments intended to establish the claim (G3), it is also the case that *Reply* I, V, and IX do not *contain* arguments intended to establish the claim (G3) because a careful reading of the *Reply* shows that while the *Reply* contains the claim that

(G4) it is necessary that the being than-which-a-greater-cannot-be-thought exists [*necesse est illud esse*] [4]

as well as (c), (d), and (e), the claim (G3) does not occur in the *Reply*. However, perhaps the claim (G4) would be an acceptable substitute for the claim (G3) in this treatment of the *Reply* which Hartshorne and Charlesworth provide. There are two objections to this suggestion. First, while *Reply* V contains a claim which uses a variation of "*necesse*" the claim (G4) does not occur in *Reply* V, and, hence, *Reply* V cannot contain an argument intended to establish the claim (G4). Second, where (G4) does occur, it is not used in the way which would be required by Hartshorne and Charlesworth in order for (G4) to be treated as the conclusion of an argument. According to the treatment of the *Reply* which Hartshorne and Charlesworth provide, in order for the claim (G3) to count as the conclusion of an argument, the claim that the being than-which-a-greater-cannot-be-thought necessarily exists must be used in such a way that the term "necessarily" both means logically necessary and is asserted as a property of the existence of the being than-which-a-greater-cannot-be-thought.

But it is not the case that (G4) is used in either *Reply* I or IX in a way such that it would satisfy these two conditions. The claim (G4) occurs three times in *Reply* I and IX, twice in *Reply* I (although a variation of the term "*necesse*," "*ex necessitate est*," also occurs in

---

[4] *Ibid.*, p. 169.

Reply I) and once in *Reply* IX. In both of its occurrences in *Reply* I, (G4) is explicitly the consequent of a hypothetical statement, and in its single occurrence in *Reply* IX (G4) is implicitly the consequent of a hypothetical statement. What Anselm is saying is that, given certain conditions, then it is necessary (logically necessary) that (*c*), (*d*), and (*e*) follow from the statement of those conditions, that (*c*), (*d*), and (*e*) are the necessary consequences of a certain set of propositions. That this is the case should be obvious from Chapters V and X of the *Reply*. In *Reply* V Anselm asserts not claim (G3) *or* claim (G4) but

> ... so also that which is greater than everything is said to be understood and to exist in the mind, and so is *necessarily inferred [ex necessitate concluditur]* to exist in reality itself.[5] (Italics mine.)

In *Reply* X Anselm says

> For the import of this proof is in itself of such force that what is spoken of is proved (as a *necessary consequence* of the fact that it is understood or thought of) both to exist in actual reality and to be itself whatever must be believed about the Divine Being.[6] (Italics mine.)

While Anselm is using the claim (G4) in such a way that the term "necessary" means logically necessary, he is *not* asserting that logical necessity is a property of the existence of the being than-which-a-greater-cannot-be-thought any more than one would be asserting that logical necessity is a property of the mortality of Socrates by asserting that if all men are mortal, then it is necessary that Socrates is mortal. What is clearly being asserted in this latter case is that the proposition that Socrates is mortal follows necessarily from the statement of certain conditions, namely, that all men are mortal and that Socrates is a man. Similarly, what Anselm is asserting in the claim (G4) is that logical necessity is a property of the relationship between (c) and the statement of certain conditions and between (d) and the statement of certain conditions and between (e) and the statement of certain conditions. In short, Anselm is simply saying that (c), (d) and (e) do in fact *follow* necessarily from a certain set of propositions. Since the claim (G4) does not satisfy the conditions required of the claim (G3) in order for the claim (G3) to be the conclusion of an argument, the claim (G4) is not an adequate

---

[5] *Ibid.*, p. 183.
[6] *Ibid.*, pp. 189-191.

substitute for the claim (G3), and since the claim (G3) does not occur in the *Reply*, *Reply* I, V, and IX cannot contain arguments intended to establish the claim (G3).

But, perhaps the view that *Reply* I, V, and IX contain arguments intended to establish the claim (G3) is not maintained on the grounds that the term "*necesse*" and its variations occur in the *Reply*. Perhaps this view is maintained either on the grounds that (d) occurs in the *Reply*, or on the grounds that (e) occurs in the *Reply*. If this view is maintained on the grounds that (d) occurs in the *Reply* then there are two objections to this view. Both of these objections hold against Hartshorne and one of them holds against Charlesworth. The first objection which holds only against Hartshorne is that (d) does not occur in *Reply* IX; and, hence, contrary to what Hartshorne would have us believe, *Reply* IX could *not* contain an argument intended to establish the claim (G3). The second objection which holds against both Hartshorne and Charlesworth is that, as we have already seen, (d) (which contains the phrase "cannot be thought not to exist") cannot be transformed in terms of logical necessity or logical possibility. Therefore, it cannot be maintained that *Reply* I, V, and IX contain arguments intended to establish the claim (G3) on the grounds that the *Reply* contains (d). If this view is maintained on the grounds that the *Reply* contains (e) (which itself contains the phrase "cannot not exist"), then the objection to this view is that there is no reason to think that Anselm intends to assert anything about *logical necessity* when he uses the phrase "cannot not exist" (*non potest non esse*). What Anselm does indicate is that something which cannot not exist is something which has no beginning and no ending, and it certainly does not follow from the assertion, that a thing has no beginning and no ending, that the existence of that thing is logically necessary. Therefore, since there are no grounds for transforming the claim (e) into the claim (G3), it cannot be maintained that *Reply* I, V, and IX contain arguments intended to establish the claim (G3) on the grounds that the *Reply* contains (e).

Accordingly, since the *Reply* is, at least in part and in some way, a defense of *Proslogion* III and since the *Reply* does not contain the claim (G3), it follows that neither *Reply* I, V, nor IX can be treated as arguments intended to establish the claim that the being than-which-a-greater-cannot-be-thought necessarily exists and that some other explanation of the *Reply* must be given in order to account for it as a defense of *Proslogion* III. But it does not follow that Chapters I, V, and IX of the *Reply* contain arguments intended to establish the claim (c)-(d)-(e). From the obvious fact that the *Reply* is, at least in part and in some way, a defense of *Proslogion* III, it does not follow, it is not an adequate explanation of the *Reply* as a defense of *Proslogion* III to say, that in the *Reply* Anselm is defending *Proslogion* III by defending the claim of *Proslogion* III. While Hartshorne and Charlesworth are, at least in part, correct in assuming that the *Reply* is a defense of *Proslogion* III, they are wrong in assuming that it is the *claim* of *Proslogion* III which is being defended in the *Reply*. In order to explain the *Reply* as a defense of *Proslogion* III, it must be recognized that the main thrust of Gaunilo's criticism of the *Proslogion* is aimed not at the claim of *Proslogion* III but at the *existential reasoning* of *Proslogion* II and III, which is itself intended to establish the claim of *Proslogion* III.

Gaunilo argues that Anselm's existential reasoning does not hold, that Anselm's claim (c)-(d)-(e) does not follow from his assumptions. Accordingly, in the *Reply* Anselm defends *not* the claim (c)-(d)-(e) but the claim that the existential reasoning of *Proslogion* II and III which establishes (c)-(d)-(e) holds. In our examination of Anselm's use of the term "*necesse*" and its variations, we have already seen that Anselm's primary claim in the *Reply* is that, given certain conditions, then (c), (d), and (e) do in fact follow from the statement of those conditions. Anselm has already established the claim (c)-(d)-(e) in *Proslogion* II and III, in the *Reply* he argues that the reasoning of *Proslogion* II and III obtains even in the face of Gaunilo's objections. The *Reply* is a defense of *Proslogion* III by virtue of the fact that it is a defense of the *reasoning* of *Proslogion* II and III.

Furthermore, the procedure which Anselm employs in the defense of his existential reasoning does not consist in providing arguments in addition to the reasoning of *Proslogion* II and III, rather, Anselm's defense consists in explicating the existential reasoning of *Proslogion* II and III in order to show that Gaunilo's criticisms of that reasoning do not hold. In fulfilling its primary function as a response to Gaunilo's criticisms, the *Reply* also serves the further and secondary function of providing a commentary on the highly compact reasoning of *Proslogion* II and III. In the process of defending the existential reasoning of *Proslogion* II and III against Gaunilo's criticisms, Anselm also fills out and makes more explicit the existential reasoning of *Proslogion* II and III. The existential reasoning of *Proslogion* II and III establishes that several existential claims can be proved about the being than-which-a-greater-cannot-be-thought while the *Reply* shows *how* it is that the reasoning of *Proslogion* II and III establishes that several existential claims can be proved about the being than-which-a-greater-cannot-be-thought.

In its secondary function the *Reply* does not constitute a piece of reasoning in addition to the existential reasoning in *Proslogion* II and III, rather, the *Reply* represents the existential reasoning of *Proslogion* II and III in commentary. But because its function as a commentary is only a secondary function the *Reply* does not constitute a systematic commentary on the existential reasoning of *Proslogion* II and III. Because Anselm's primary aim in the *Reply* was to answer Gaunilo's objections to the reasoning of *Proslogion* II and III, Anselm did not provide a systematic or organized explication of his reasoning in *Proslogion* II and III. The result of this is that the several distinct portions of the *Reply* must be reorganized by reference to the reasoning of *Proslogion* II and III in order to derive the full benefit of the *Reply* as a commentary on the reasoning of *Proslogion* II and III.

In short, what it is in the *Proslogion* which Anselm defends in the *Reply* is the existential reasoning of *Proslogion* II and III, and the procedure which Anselm employs in his defense of the *Proslogion* consists in explicating the existential reasoning of *Proslogion* II and III. The significance of the *Reply* to the existential reasoning of *Proslogion* II and III is that the *Reply* provides a commentary on the highly compact existential reasoning of *Proslogion* II and III. The next task, then, is to examine *Proslogion* II and *Proslogion* III in the light of Anselm's commentary on these two Chapters in the *Reply* and to organize Anselm's commentary in the *Reply* by reference to the existential reasoning of *Proslogion* II and III in order to determine as precisely as possible what Anselm's reasoning is in *Proslogion* II and III.

The Basis for the Deduction of Anselm's Existential Claims

When we turn to *Proslogion* II and III, the most important problem is to discover what Anselm is asserting in his second sentence of the reasoning of *Proslogion* II when he says that if it exists solely in the mind even, it can be thought to exist in reality also, which is greater. Understanding this second sentence of the reasoning of *Proslogion* II is manifestly the key to determining precisely what Anselm's existential reasoning is in *Proslogion* II and III. In fact, a careful reading of *Proslogion* II and III should make it plain that it is Anselm's second sentence of the reasoning of *Proslogion* II which constitutes the core of his existential reasoning and that this second sentence needs to be unpacked in order to determine what set of propositions it is which constitutes Anselm's basis for the deduction of his existential claims (c), (d), and (e). But what exactly is Anselm asserting in his second sentence, and most particularly, what exactly is Anselm asserting in the subordinate clause "which is greater" (*quod majus est*)? According to the proponents of the current interpretations, at least part of what Anselm is asserting in this second sentence is (h), that existence in reality is greater than existence in the mind alone. Unfortunately no justification is ever given for thinking that Anselm would subscribe to assertion (h) as even a partial interpretation of his second sentence, and while it is impossible to prove that Anselm would reject (h), I argued in my previous chapter that Anselm is not committed to assertion (h). The status, then, of assertion (h) is undecided. It is possible that Anselm might subscribe to assertion (h) and it is possible that Anselm might reject assertion (h). Accordingly, it is not at all immediately obvious how Anselm's second sentence is to be interpreted.

However, while it is not immediately obvious what Anselm is asserting in his second sentence, it would seem to be clear that two general sets of conditions must be satisfied by any adequate interpretation of Anselm's second sentence. First, no matter how this second sentence is interpreted, that interpretation must not be made *in vacuo*. Any adequate interpretation of this second sentence must be determined and suggested by the total context in which it occurs. If an interpretation of this second sentence is to be counted as adequate, then it must constitute a set of propositions having certain characteristics. To be counted as adequate, an interpretation of this second sentence must constitute a set of propositions having characteristics which can be shown to be required by such contextual considerations as Anselm's general methodology or procedure, the claims that can be determined to be true about the being which is the subject of Anselm's reasoning, and the other claims which Anselm makes both in *Proslogion* II and III and the *Reply*. Second, no matter how this second sentence is interpreted, that interpretation must constitute a set of propositions from which (c), (d), and (e) are all deducible, or at least a set of propositions from which (c), (d), and (e) could be reasonably thought to be deducible, and it must constitute a set of propositions which provides grounds for a reasonable explanation of Anselm's single-argument claim. Any interpretation of Anselm's second sentence is certainly inadequate if it does not at least give the appearance of being sufficient to support the deduction of (c), (d), and (e), and any interpretation of Anselm's second sentence is certainly inadequate if it has the result that Anselm's existential deductions would be completely independent of his theistic deductions. Surely then, an interpretation of Anselm's second sentence which does *not* satisfy these general conditions must be regarded as an inadequate interpretation, and an interpretation which *does* satisfy these general conditions must, in lieu of a still stronger interpretation, be regarded as an adequate interpretation. The present task, then, is to determine as precisely as possible what Anselm's existential reasoning is in *Proslogion* II and III by finding an interpretation of Anselm's second sentence which satisfies these general conditions of adequacy.

Now, because of the possibility that Anselm *might* subscribe to assertion (h) even though he is not committed to assertion (h), it is possible that there may be an interpretation of Anselm's second sentence which constitutes a set of propositions containing (h) as one of its constituents such that the set of propositions as a whole has characteristics which can be shown to be required by relevant contextual considerations and such that the set of propositions provides sufficient grounds for the deduction of (c), (d), and (e) and provides grounds for a reasonable explanation of Anselm's single-argument claim. But while the possibility of such an interpretation is not precluded by anything that is now known, it is equally true that there is nothing that has yet been determined which would suggest that there is an interpretation of Anselm's second sentence which constitutes a set of propositions containing (h) as one of its constituents and satisfying the general conditions of adequacy. In short, in finding an interpretation of Anselm's second sentence, there is no obligation to find a set of propositions containing (h) as one of its constituents.

In finding an interpretation of Anselm's second sentence, the only obligation is to find a set of propositions which can be justified as representing the basis for Anselm's series of existential deductions on the grounds that the set of propositions satisfies the general conditions of adequacy. As a matter of fact, when the relevant contextual considerations are examined, it turns out that there is an interpretation of Anselm's second sentence constituting a set of propositions which satisfies the general conditions of adequacy but which does not contain (h) as one of its constituent propositions. The procedure for developing this interpretation will consist in examining certain relevant contextual considerations. From an examination of these contextual considerations it will be possible to determine what characteristics those contextual considerations specify that must be exemplified by Anselm's set of propositions constituting the basis for his series of existential deductions. It will then be possible to unpack Anselm's second sentence by transforming this sentence in such a way as to exemplify those characteristics which the examination of the contextual considerations has determined as the characteristics which must be exemplified by Anselm's set of propositions constituting the basis for his series of existential deductions.

A consideration of Anselm's general methodology or procedure makes it plain that Anselm is arguing for the general claim that if the being than-which-a-greater-cannot-be-thought does *not* exist in reality, then a contradiction arises about the being than-which-a-greater-cannot-be-thought. More explicitly Anselm is arguing for the general claim that if the being than-which-a-greater-cannot-be-thought does *not* exist in reality, then certain conditions obtain such that a contradiction arises about the being than-which-a-greater-cannot-be-thought, and, hence, at least one of those conditions and whatever implies it cannot obtain. It is equally obvious that it is Anselm's second sentence of the reasoning of *Proslogion* II which is intended both to indicate what the conditions are that lead to the contradiction and to indicate the basis for the contradiction which is supposed to arise if those conditions obtain. In order to find an adequate interpretation of Anselm's second sentence, then, it is necessary to determine two things. It is necessary to determine what the context suggests to be the nature of the contradiction which arises if certain conditions obtain, and it is necessary to determine what the context suggests to be the nature of the conditions which lead to this contradiction.

Now, the contradiction which Anselm has in mind is a contradiction specifically concerning the being than-which-a-greater-cannot-be-thought. The nature of the contradiction, then, will depend upon the nature of this being and the claims that can be determined to be true about this being by virtue of its nature. Anselm characterized this being as

> *aliquid quo majus nihil cogitari potest*,[7]

or alternatively

> *id quo majus cogitari non potest*,[8]

translated respectively as

> something than which nothing greater can be thought

and

> something than which a greater cannot be thought.

So, presumably, what Anselm means by 'the being than-which-a-greater-cannot-be-thought' is

> (T) Something, x, such that nothing can be thought to be greater than x.

But the phrase "nothing can be thought to be greater than x" is elliptical like the phrase "nobody is taller than Joe." When this latter phrase is made more explicit, it means something like "nobody's height is greater than Joe's height." Similarly, when (T) is made more explicit, it means something like

> (T1) Something, x, such that nothing can be thought to have a degree of greatness greater than the degree of greatness which x has.

However, (T1) needs some modification. Superficially at least (T1) seems to imply, by itself, that x exists because if x has anything, whether it be some degree of greatness or some other property, then x exists. Anselm handles this problem by distinguishing between existence *in re* and existence *in intellectu*. What Anselm means by 'the being than-which-a-greater-cannot-be-thought' is

> (T2) Something, x, such that nothing can be thought to have a degree of greatness greater than the degree of greatness which x has *in intellectu*.

Furthermore, since, for Anselm, existence *in intellectu* consists in

---
[7] *Ibid.*, p. 116.
[8] *Ibid.*

being understood or thought, then to have some degree of greatness *in intellectu* is to be thought to have some degree of greatness. Accordingly, what Anselm means by 'the being than-which-a-greater-cannot-be-thought' is

> (T3) Something, x, such that nothing can be thought to have a degree of greatness greater than the degree of greatness which x can be thought to have,

or more simply

> (T4) Something, x, such that nothing can be thought to be greater than x can be thought to be.

By virtue of what we have so far discovered Anselm to mean by 'the being than-which-a-greater-cannot-be-thought,' the claim would seem to be true about this being that nothing can be thought to be greater than this being can be thought to be. If this claim is true, then it must also be true that this being cannot be thought to be greater than itself from one time to another because if the being itself can be thought at one time by virtue of some feature to be greater than it is thought to be at another time, then some other thing could be thought to have that feature and could, hence, be thought to be greater than the being which is such that nothing can be thought to be greater than it can be thought to be. In its most explicit form, what Anselm means by 'the being than-which-a-greater-cannot-be-thought' is:

> (T5) Something, x, such that for *any* time t and for *any* y if x is thought at t then there is *no* time -t prior to t and there is *no* time +t subsequent to t such that x or y can at -t or +t be thought to be greater than x can be thought at t to be.

It would seem, then, that (T5) is a complete determination of the nature of the being than-which-a-greater-cannot-be-thought and that the claim which can be determined to be true about this being by virtue of its nature is the claim that

> (M) It is false that something can be thought to be greater than the being than-which-a-greater-cannot-be-thought can be thought to be.

Now, the denial of (M)

(N) Something can be thought to be greater than the being than-which-a-greater-cannot-be-thought can be thought to be

is self-contradictory; and if something could by virtue of some feature be thought to be greater than the being than-which-a-greater-cannot-be-thought can be thought to be, then *anything*, including the being itself, could be thought to have that feature and could, hence, be thought to be greater than the being than-which-a-greater-cannot-be-thought can be thought to be. Because of this and because a contradiction implies anything, (N) implies

(N1) Anything can be thought to be greater than the being than-which-a-greater-cannot-be-thought can be thought to be

and surely (N1) describes the nature of the contradiction which Anselm claims would arise if certain conditions obtain. But since the conditions which would lead to the contradiction are conditions which would obtain if the being than-which-a-greater-cannot-be-thought does not exist in reality and those conditions are conditions which would obtain for the being than-which-a-greater-cannot-be-thought, the specific contradiction which Anselm has in mind is

(J) The being than-which-a-greater-cannot-be-thought can be thought to be greater than the being than-which-a-greater-cannot-be-thought can be thought to be,

and (J) can, according to (T5), be read as

(J1) The being than-which-a-greater-cannot-be-thought can at t be thought to be greater than it can be thought at t' to be

or, in its abbreviated form,

(j) The being than-which-a-greater-cannot-be-thought can be thought to be greater.

In addition, since Anselm's claim is that the contradiction (j) arises from certain conditions which would obtain for the being than-which-a-greater-cannot-be-thought if this being does not exist in reality, it is clear that at least some of those conditions must be conditions of thought about the being and that the justification for the contradiction (j) must be that thinking the being in one way is thinking it to be greater than thinking it in another way. What Anselm is claiming, then, is that there are certain conditions of thought such that thinking the being than-which-a-greater-cannot-be-thought in the first way is thinking it to be greater than thinking it in the second way, that if the being than-which-a-greater-cannot-be-thought does not exist in reality then certain conditions obtain for this being including those conditions of thought, and that if those conditions of thought obtain for this being then the contradiction (j) arises. Accordingly, at least part of what Anselm is saying in his second sentence of the reasoning of *Proslogion* II is

(P) If the being than-which-a-greater-cannot-be-thought can at t′ be thought as it could be thought if it exists in the mind alone and the being than-which-a-greater-cannot-be-thought can at t be thought to exist in reality, then the being than-which-a-greater-cannot-be-thought can at t be thought to be greater than it can be thought at t′ to be

(where the consequent of this conditional means "the being can at t be thought to have a greatness greater than *some greatness* it can be thought at t′ to have" as distinguished from "the being can at t be thought to have a greatness greater than *any greatness* it can be thought at t′ to have") as well as

(l) The being than-which-a-greater-cannot-be-thought can be thought to exist in reality.

But how is (P) to be unpacked ? How is it that this being could be thought if it exists in the mind alone ? Since the statement

(k) The being than-which-a-greater-cannot-be-thought exists in the mind alone

is equivalent in Anselm's doctrine to

(k′) The being than-which-a-greater-cannot-be-thought does not exist in reality,

the question of how it is that this being could be thought if it exists in the mind alone is equivalent to the question of how it is that this being could be thought if it does not exist in reality. An answer to the latter question would constitute an answer to the former question and conversely. Furthermore, an answer to either of these questions would indicate both what the further conditions of thought about this being are which would lead to the contradiction (j) and what other conditions Anselm thinks would obtain for the being than-which-a-greater-cannot-be-thought if the being does not exist in reality. There are two textual considerations which would indicate what these conditions are. In the third sentence of the reasoning of *Proslogion* II, Anselm claims

> If then that-than-which-a-greater-cannot-be-thought exists in the mind alone, this same that-than-which-a-greater-*cannot*-be-thought is that-than-which-a-greater-*can*-be-thought,[9]

and in the third sentence of *Proslogion* III Anselm claims

> Hence, if that-than-which-a-greater-cannot-be-thought can be thought not to exist, then that-than-which-a-greater-cannot-be-thought is not the same as that-than-which-a-greater-cannot-be-thought...[10]

In *Proslogion* II Anselm claims that the contradiction arises about the being than-which-a-greater-cannot-be-thought if the being exists in the mind alone (i.e., if it does not exist in reality). In *Proslogion* III Anselm claims that the contradiction arises about the being than-which-a-greater-cannot-be-thought if the being can be *thought* not to exist (presumably in reality). So, if we take *Proslogion* II and *Proslogion* III together in order to further unpack the second sentence of the reasoning of *Proslogion* II, then it would seem that Anselm is saying that if the being than-which-a-greater-cannot-be-thought does not exist in reality, then the being than-which-a-greater-cannot-be-thought can be *thought* not to exist in reality. The way that this being can be thought if it does not exist in reality is that it can be *thought* not to exist in reality. At least one of the conditions which obtains for the being than-which-a-greater-cannot-be-thought if it does not exist in reality is the condition of thought that it can be *thought* not to exist in reality. Accordingly, at least part of what Anselm is saying in the second sentence of the reasoning of *Proslogion* II is

> (P′)   If the being than-which-a-greater-cannot-be-thought can at t′ be thought not to exist in reality and the being than-which-a-greater-cannot-be-thought can at t be thought to exist in reality, then the being than-which-a-greater-

---

[9] *Ibid.*, p. 117.
[10] *Ibid.*, p. 119.

cannot-be-thought can at t be thought to be greater than it can be thought at t′ to be

as well as

(l) The being than-which-a-greater-cannot-be-thought can be thought to exist in reality.

If there is any question as to whether or not Anselm is really asserting the connection between the existence of this being and what can be thought about this being which has been justified by taking *Proslogion* II and *Proslogion* III together, then it is only necessary to examine one of Anselm's claims in *Reply* V in order to see that Anselm explicitly asserts that connection. In *Reply* V Anselm enunciates the principle that

(RV) What does not exist can possibly not exist, and what can not exist can be thought of as not existing.[11]

When (RV) is instantiated with respect to the being than-which-a-greater-cannot-be-thought, (RV) makes explicit at least part of what is implicit in the second sentence of the reasoning of *Proslogion* II. When it is instantiated, (RV) makes explicit at least some of the conditions which Anselm thinks would obtain for the being than-which-a-greater-cannot-be-thought if the being does not exist in reality, and it shows that *at least* one of those conditions is a condition which specifies what can be thought about this being if it does not exist in reality. What Anselm is saying is that if the being than-which-a-greater-cannot-be-thought does not exist in reality, then it can possibly not exist in reality and if the being than-which-a-greater-cannot-be-thought can possibly not exist in reality then it can be thought not to exist in reality. So, at least part of what Anselm asserts in the second sentence of the reasoning of *Proslogion* II is (P′), stated in a more abbreviated form as

(P4) If the being than-which-a-greater-cannot-be-thought can be thought not to exist in reality and the being than-which-a-greater-cannot-be-thought can be thought to exist in reality, then the being than-which-a-greater-cannot-be-thought can be thought to be greater

as well as

---

[11] *Ibid.*, p. 179.

(P5) The being than-which-a-greater-cannot-be-thought can be thought to exist in reality

and (P4), when taken together with the equivalence of (k) to (k′) and the instantiation of (RV), implies

(S) If the being than-which-a-greater-cannot-be-thought exists in the mind alone and the being than-which-a-greater-cannot-be-thought can be thought to exist in reality, then the being than-which-a-greater-cannot-be-thought can be thought to be greater

where (S) contains the original predicates of Anselm's second sentence, "exists in the mind alone" and "can be thought to exist in reality."

But (P4) and (P5) are not all that Anselm asserts in the second sentence of the reasoning of *Proslogion* II. When Anselm's second sentence of the reasoning of *Proslogion* II is still further unpacked by reference to the principle (RV) which Anselm enunciates in *Reply* V, then the second sentence of the reasoning of *Proslogion* II constitutes the basis for his series of existential deductions in *Proslogion* II and III about the being than-which-a-greater-cannot-be-thought. In its preliminary formulation, Anselm's basis for his series of existential deductions, the explicit formulation of what is implicit in Anselm's second sentence of the reasoning of *Proslogion* II, can be represented in the following way:

(P1) If the being than-which-a-greater-cannot-be-thought exists in the mind alone, then it does not exist in reality.

(P2) If the being than-which-a-greater-cannot-be-thought does not exist in reality, then it can not exist [i.e., can fail to exist] in reality.

(P3) If the being than-which-a-greater-cannot-be-thought can not exist in reality, then it can be thought not to exist in reality.

(P4) If the being than-which-a-greater-cannot-be-thought can be thought not to exist in reality and the being than-which-a-greater-cannot-be-thought can be thought to exist in reality, then the being than-which-a-greater-cannot-be-thought can be thought to be greater.

(P5) The being than-which-a-greater-cannot-be-thought can be thought to exist in reality.

When it is unpacked, Anselm's second sentence of the reasoning of *Proslogion* II is represented in its preliminary formulation by (P1) through (P5), and since Anselm assumes

    (P6)   It is false that the being than-which-a-greater-cannot-be-thought can be thought to be greater,

(P1) through (P6) represents the basis for Anselm's series of existential deductions about the being than-which-a-greater-cannot-be-thought.

Now, before we discuss the question of whether or not (c)-(d)-(e) is deducible from the basis which Anselm provides for the deduction of this series of existential claims, it is necessary to first determine what is the *final* formulation of Anselm's basis for his series of existential deductions about the being than-which-a-greater-cannot-be-thought. In order to determine this final formulation, it is necessary to examine (P4). At first glance it might be thought that (P4) has its basis in assertion (h); that is, it might be thought that (P4) rests on the assumption that existence in reality is greater than existence in the mind alone on the grounds that the contradiction in (P4) must be justified by the claim that:

    (P4')   Thinking the being than-which-a-greater-cannot-be-thought to exist in reality is thinking it to be greater than thinking it not to exist in reality

and that (P4') implies

    (h')   Existing in reality is greater than not existing in reality

where (h') is equivalent to (h). In short, it might be argued that (P4) commits Anselm to assertion (h) after all. But this argument does *not* show that Anselm is committed to assertion (h) because while it is true that (P4') implies (h') and (h') implies (h) and while it is true that the contradiction in (P4) must be justified by a claim of the form that thinking the being in one way is thinking it to be greater than thinking it in another way and while it is true that the contradiction in (P4) *could* be justified by the claim (P4') that thinking the being to exist in reality is thinking it to be greater than thinking it not to exist in reality, it is *not* true that the contradiction in (P4) *must* be justified by the claim (P4'). In order to hold that Anselm *is* committed to assertion (h), it would be necessary to provide at least one reason for thinking that the claim (P4') constitutes Anselm's justification for the contradiction in (P4). If Anselm asserted (P4'), then that would be a good reason for thinking that Anselm would justify the contradiction in (P4) by the claim (P4'), or if Anselm asserted some other proposition that implies or is even just implied by (P4'), then that would provide a good reason for thinking that Anselm would justify the contradiction in (P4) by the claim (P4'). For example, since (h') is implied by (P4') even though (h') does not imply (P4'), then if Anselm asserted (h'), that would be a good reason to suppose that Anselm justifies the contradiction in (P4) by the claim (P4'); but Anselm does not assert (P4') nor any proposition which implies or is implied by (P4'), and he most certainly does not assert (h'). In fact, if Anselm did assert (h'), there would be no need to argue that (P4) commits Anselm to assertion (h) because (h') is equivalent to (h). So, while (P4') implies (h') and, hence, assertion (h) and while Anselm's methodology as well as *Reply* III suggests that the contradiction in (P4) is certainly justified by a further claim, there is no reason to think that Anselm would justify the contradiction in (P4) by the claim (P4'); and, hence, there is no reason to suppose that Anselm is committed to assertion (h).

What Anselm's methodology and *Reply* III suggest is that (P4) is derived from three other propositions which further constitute a part of Anselm's basis for his series of existential deductions and that the contradiction is justified by a claim other than (P4'). Anselm's methodology is to claim that if the being than-which-a-greater-cannot-be-thought does not exist in reality, then certain conditions, specified by (RV), obtain which lead to the contradiction; and when we consult *Reply* III, we find that Anselm identifies a further condition of thought which obtains for the being than-which-a-greater-cannot-be-thought if it does not exist in reality. In *Reply* III Anselm claims that

(F4) If the being than-which-a-greater-cannot-be-thought can be thought not to exist in reality, then it can be thought to have a beginning and an end;

and although he does not assert it explicitly, presumably the claim

(F5) If the being than-which-a-greater-cannot-be-thought can be thought to exist in reality, then it can be thought not to have a beginning or an end

also holds on Anselm's view; and since (P4) is implied by these two propositions and

(F6) If the being than-which-a-greater-cannot-be-thought can be thought to have a beginning and an end and the being than-which-a-greater-cannot-be-thought can be thought not to have a beginning or an end, then the being than-which-a-greater-cannot-be-thought can be thought to be greater,

then Anselm's methodology and *Reply* III suggest that for Anselm (P4) is derived from (F4), (F5), and (F6). What Anselm is claiming is that if the being than-which-a-greater-cannot-be-thought does not exist in reality, then certain conditions would obtain for this being which would lead to the contradiction (j), and Anselm's methodology and *Reply* III suggest that (F4) and (F5) further specify what those conditions are and that (F4), (F5), and (F6) constitute a further part of the basis for his series of existential deductions. Now the contradiction in (F6) can be justified by the claim that

(F6′) Thinking the being than-which-a-greater-cannot-be-thought not to have a beginning or an end is thinking it to be greater than thinking it to have a beginning and an end,

and although Anselm does not explicitly assert (F6′), (F6′) does imply

(n) Having no beginning or end is greater than having a beginning and an end;

and Anselm explicitly asserts (n) in *Reply* VIII when he says

> Who, for example, cannot think of this...namely, that if something that has a beginning and end is good, that which, although it has had a beginning, does not, however, have an end, is much better? And just as this latter is better than the former, so also that which has neither beginning nor end is better again than this...[12]

So, since the claim (F6′) implies (n) and Anselm explicitly asserts (n), assertion (n) provides a good reason for further thinking that (F4), (F5), and (F6) are part of Anselm's basis for his series of existential deductions and for thinking that (F6′) is Anselm's justification for the contradiction which he claims arises if the being than-which-a-greater-cannot-be-thought does not exist in reality. Accordingly, it is

---

[12] *Ibid.*, p. 187.

(n), not (h), which is for Anselm the most basic and fundamental principle of his existential reasoning and since (F6′) implies (n), even though (n) does not imply (F6′), and since (P4) is implied by (F4), (F5), and (F6), even though Anselm does not explicitly assert (F5) or (F6), it is not unreasonable or farfetched to interpret Anselm as asserting (F5) and (F6) as part of his basis for his series of existential deductions and as holding the claim (F6′) as the justification for the contradiction in (F6).

In its final formulation Anselm's basis for his series of existential deductions about the being than-which-a-greater-cannot-be-thought can be represented in the following way:

(F1) If the being than-which-a-greater-cannot-be-thought exists in the mind alone, then it does not exist in reality.

(F2) If the being than-which-a-greater-cannot-be-thought does not exist in reality, then it can not exist [i.e., can fail to exist] in reality.

(F3) If the being than-which-a-greater-cannot-be-thought can not exist in reality, then it can be thought not to exist in reality.

(F4) If the being than-which-a-greater-cannot-be-thought can be thought not to exist in reality, then it can be thought to have a beginning and an end.

(F5) If the being than-which-a-greater-cannot-be-thought can be thought to exist in reality, then it can be thought not to have a beginning or an end.

(F6) If the being than-which-a-greater-cannot-be-thought can be thought to have a beginning and an end and the being than-which-a-greater-cannot-be-thought can be thought not to have a beginning or an end, then the being than-which-a-greater-cannot-be-thought can be thought to be greater.

(F7) The being than-which-a-greater-cannot-be-thought can be thought to exist in reality.

(F8) It is false that the being than-which-a-greater-cannot-be-thought can be thought to be greater.

Now, (F1) through (F7) represents the expansion of Anselm's second sentence of the reasoning of *Proslogion* II, which was achieved by interpreting Anselm's second sentence in the light of his own methodology and his assertions in *Proslogion* III and the *Reply*, and

Anselm's second sentence can be derived from (F1) through (F7). In order to show this, we first let the following letters stand as abbreviations for the statements which follow them:

(k) The being than-which-a-greater-cannot-be-thought exists in the mind alone.

(c) The being than-which-a-greater-cannot-be-thought exists in reality.

(o) The being than-which-a-greater-cannot-be-thought can not exist [i.e., can fail to exist] in reality.

(m) The being than-which-a-greater-cannot-be-thought can be thought not to exist in reality.

(p) The being than-which-a-greater-cannot-be-thought can be thought to have a beginning and an end.

(l) The being than-which-a-greater-cannot-be-thought can be thought to exist in reality.

(q) The being than-which-a-greater-cannot-be-thought can be thought not to have a beginning or an end.

(j) The being than-which-a-greater-cannot-be-thought can be thought to be greater.

Next we symbolize (F1) through (F8) in the following way:

(D1) CkNc
(D2) CNco
(D3) Com
(D4) Cmp
(D5) Clq
(D6) CKpqj
(D7) l
(D8) Nj

Now, since Anselm's second sentence of the reasoning of *Proslogion* II asserts (S) and (l), then Anselm's second sentence can be symbolized as KCKkljl, and this latter formula can be deduced from (D1) through (D8) in the following way:

(S1) CKqpj   (from (D6) by Commutation)
(S2) CqCpj   (from (S1) by Exportation)
(S3) ClCpj   (from (D5) and (S2) by Hypothetical Syllogism)
(S4) CKlpj   (from (S3) by Exportation)
(S5) CKplj   (from (S4) by Commutation)
(S6) CpClj   (from (S5) by Exportation)
(S7) Cko   (from (D1) and (D2) by Hypothetical Syllogism)
(S8) Ckm   (from (S7) and (D3) by Hypothetical Syllogism)

(S9)	Ckp	(from (S8) and (D4) by Hypothetical Syllogism)
(S10)	CkClj	(from (S9) and (S6) by Hypothetical Syllogism)
(S11)	CKklj	(from (S10) by Exportation)
(S12)	KCKkljl	(from (S11) and (D7) by Conjunction)

Hence, since KCKkljl asserts:

> If the being than-which-a-greater-cannot-be-thought exists in the mind alone and the being than-which-a-greater-cannot-be-thought can be thought to exist in reality, then the being than-which-a-greater-cannot-be-thought can be thought to be greater; and the being than-which-a-greater-cannot-be-thought *can* be thought to exist in reality,

then Anselm's second sentence of the reasoning of *Proslogion* II can be derived from (F1) through (F7), and (F1) through (F8) can be reasonably regarded as faithfully representing Anselm's basis for his series of existential deductions about the being than-which-a-greater-cannot-be-thought.

Anselm's Existential Reasoning in Proslogion II and III

When we take the reasoning of *Proslogion* II and the reasoning of *Proslogion* III together and interpret it in the light of Anselm's commentary on that reasoning in the *Reply*, it turns out that (F1) through (F8) constitutes the basis for Anselm's series of existential deductions (c), (d), and (e). In *Proslogion* II Anselm is claiming and attempting to show that (c) is deducible from the basis (F1) through (F8), and in *Proslogion* III Anselm is claiming and attempting to show that (d) and (e) are also deducible from the basis (F1) through (F8). Given the symbolized form of (F1) through (F8); that is, given:

(D1)	CkNc
(D2)	CNco
(D3)	Com
(D4)	Cmp
(D5)	Clq
(D6)	CKpqj
(D7)	l
(D8)	Nj

then Anselm's existential reasoning of *Proslogion* II, the deduction of (c) from (F1) through (F8), can be represented in the following series of deductions:

(D9)   CKqpj   (from (D6) by Commutation)
(D10) CqCpj   (from (D9) by Exportation)
(D11) ClCpj   (from (D5) and (D10) by Hypothetical Syllogism)
(D12) CKlpj   (from (D11) by Exportation)
(D13) CKplj   (from (D12) by Commutation)
(D14) CpClj   (from (D13) by Exportation)
(D15) CNcm   (from (D2) and (D3) by Hypothetical Syllogism)
(D16) CNcp   (from (D15) and (D4) by Hypothetical Syllogism)
(D17) CNcClj   (from (D16) and (D14) by Hypothetical Syllogism)
(D18) CKNclj   (from (D17) by Exportation)
(D19) CKlNcj   (from (D18) by Commutation)
(D20) ClCNcj   (from (D19) by Exportation)
(D21) CNcj   (from (D20) and (D7) by *Modus Ponens*)
(D22) c   (from (D21) and (D8) by *Modus Tollens*)

and since Nm is equivalent to (d) and No is equivalent to (e), then Anselm's existential reasoning of *Proslogion* III, the deduction of (d) from (F1) through (F8) and the deduction of (e) from (F1) through (F8), can be represented by the deductions:

(D23) Cpj   (from (D11) and (D7) by *Modus Ponens*)
(D24) Cmj   (from (D4) and (D23) by Hypothetical Syllogism)
(D25) Coj   (from (D3) and (D24) by Hypothetical Syllogism)
(D26) Nm   (from (D24) and (D8) by *Modus Tollens*)
(D27) No   (from (D25) and (D8) by *Modus Tollens*).

Consequently, when the reasoning of *Proslogion* II and the reasoning of *Proslogion* III are taken together, it can be validly deduced that

(c) the being than-which-a-greater-cannot-be-thought exists in reality,

(d) the being than-which-a-greater-cannot-be-thought cannot be thought not to exist,

and

(e) the being than-which-a-greater-cannot-be-thought cannot not exist

where (e) means for Anselm, not (G3) but

(e') the being than-which-a-greater-cannot-be-thought has neither a beginning nor an end.

It is (D1) through (D27) which represents Anselm's existential reasoning of *Proslogion* II and III, and that reasoning is beyond question formally valid. If Anselm's existential reasoning is to be criticized, then it must be on grounds other than formal validity. But before we evaluate Anselm's existential reasoning, it is perhaps advisable first to consider several questions about the relationship between what we have now identified as Anselm's existential reasoning and certain details of *Proslogion* II, *Proslogion* III, the *Reply*, and Anselm's overall program in the *Proslogion*.

How Proslogion II and III are Taken Together

We have already seen that the reasoning of *Proslogion* II and the reasoning of *Proslogion* III are dependent upon one another. Since the reasoning of *Proslogion* II alone is not logically complete and since the reasoning of *Proslogion* III alone is not logically complete, the reasoning of *Proslogion* II and the reasoning of *Proslogion* III are taken together to form the basis for a series of existential deductions about Anselm's being. Accordingly, the first question to be considered is in what way are the reasoning of *Proslogion* II and the reasoning of *Proslogion* III taken together? The answer to this question should by now be fairly clear.

The reasoning of *Proslogion* II and the reasoning of *Proslogion* III are taken together by supplying from the reasoning of *Proslogion* III at least part of the suppressed or missing premises of the reasoning of *Proslogion* II. The reasoning of *Proslogion* III provides at least part of what is suppressed or missing from the premises of the reasoning of *Proslogion* II such that when all that is suppressed or missing is made explicit, two distinct steps in a series of deductions can be made from that set of premises. Since it is what can be *thought* about the being than-which-a-greater-cannot-be-thought which determines whether or not the contradiction (j) arises, the premises of Anselm's existential reasoning of *Proslogion* II are filled out by reference to what he mentions in the reasoning of *Proslogion* III that can be *thought* about the being than-which-a-greater-cannot-be-thought. The reasoning of *Proslogion* II contains the proposition "the being than-which-a-greater-cannot-be-thought *can be thought* to exist in reality" and so the reasoning of *Proslogion* II suggests that it is this proposition which is the proposition that links the premises of the reasoning of *Proslogion* II with the reasoning of *Proslogion* III. The reasoning of *Proslogion* III contains the proposition "the being than-which-a-greater-cannot-be-thought *can be thought not* to exist (in reality)," and so the reasoning of *Proslogion* III suggests that it is this proposition which is the proposition that links the reasoning of *Proslogion* III with the premises of the reasoning of *Proslogion* II.

Between the reasoning of *Proslogion* II and the reasoning of *Proslogion* III, and so presumably within the reasoning of *Proslogion* II and within the reasoning of *Proslogion* III, Anselm contrasts the proposition "the being than-which-a-greater-cannot-be-thought *can be thought* to exist in reality" with the proposition "the being than-which-a-greater-cannot-be-thought *can be thought not* to exist (in reality)." Accordingly, the premises of the reasoning of *Proslogion* II are filled out in such a way that they contain both of these propositions. The reasoning of *Proslogion* II and the reasoning of *Proslogion* III are taken together as providing a common set of premises which contain both of these propositions referring to what can be *thought* about Anselm's being such that the reasoning of *Proslogion* II represents one step in a series of deductions from that common set of premises and such that the reasoning of *Proslogion* III represents another step in that series of deductions from that common set of premises.

The Second Sentence of the Reasoning of Proslogion III

In my second chapter we saw that the second sentence of the reasoning of *Proslogion* III cannot be treated as a premise in a logically complete and independent argument because it asserts part of what is to be proved in the conclusion (c)-(d)-(e). Accordingly, the second question to be considered is: how does the third or alternative interpretation explain the second sentence of the reasoning of *Proslogion* III? If we recall that the second sentence of the reasoning of *Proslogion* III asserts both that

(ii) Something, x, can be thought to exist and cannot be thought not to exist

and that

(iii) x is greater than what can be thought not to exist

and if we recall that for Anselm the term "the being than-which-a-greater-cannot-be-thought" is the only term that can be substituted for x in (ii) and (iii) which yield true statements then it turns out that Anselm regarded these two assertions as following from his reasoning rather than as being original premises in a logically complete and independent argument and that these two assertions function to indicate how (c)-(d)-(e) is to be deduced in the reasoning of *Proslogion* II and III. In fact, once the appropriate substitutions are made the equivalent (ii′) of (ii) follows formally from Anselm's reasoning by conjoining (D7) and (D26) because such a conjunction asserts that

> the being than-which-a-greater-cannot-be-thought can be thought to exist in reality and the being than-which-a-greater-cannot-be-thought cannot be thought not to exist in reality.

And, although (iii) does not follow formally from Anselm's premises because these premises are about only the being than-which-a-greater-cannot-be-thought, the equivalent (iii′) of (iii), namely,

> something-than-which-a-greater-cannot-be-thought is greater than what can be thought not to exist

presumably does follow from Anselm's general principle (n) and his principles about the relationship of thought to reality *because* the being than-which-a-greater-cannot-be-thought *is* the being that cannot be thought not to exist.

For, if some being can be thought not to exist, then it follows that the being than-which-a-greater-cannot-be-thought is greater than this other being because if this other being can be thought not to exist, then it can be thought to have a beginning and an end; and, presumably, if it can be thought to have a beginning and an end then it has a beginning and an end. But since having no beginning and no end is greater than having a beginning and an end and since the being than-which-a-greater-cannot-be-thought has neither a beginning nor an end and, hence, cannot be thought not to exist, it follows that the being than-which-a-greater-cannot-be-thought is greater than this other being which can be thought not to exist because it has a beginning and an end. In short, the second sentence of the reasoning of *Proslogion* III is regarded by Anselm as a consequence of, not an original premise in, his reasoning and it functions to indicate how (c)-(d)-(e) is to be deduced in the reasoning of *Proslogion* II and III from claims about what can be *thought* about Anselm's being.

The Relationship Between Reply I, V, and IX
And Anselm's Existential Reasoning

In the beginning of this present chapter I pointed out that while the *Reply* was obviously intended to serve the primary function of providing a response to Gaunilo's criticisms of the reasoning of *Proslogion* II and III, it also obviously serves the secondary function of providing a commentary on the reasoning of *Proslogion* II and III. However, despite the obviousness of this secondary function, Charlesworth has treated the differences between the reasoning of *Proslogion* III and the reasoning of *Reply* I and the differences between the reasoning of *Proslogion* III and the reasoning of *Reply* V as differences between an original argument and versions in addition to that original argument, and Hartshorne has treated these differences plus the differences between the reasoning of *Proslogion* III and the reasoning of *Reply* IX in the same general way.

But because of the fact that none of the parts of the *Reply* could represent versions of the *Proslogion* III argument on the grounds that *Proslogion* III does not contain a logically complete and independent argument, the third or alternative interpretation which takes the reasoning of *Proslogion* II and the reasoning of *Proslogion* III together treats the differences between the reasoning of *Proslogion* II and III and the reasoning of the *Reply* as differences between the original reasoning and a commentary on that reasoning. The third or alternative interpretation treats the *Reply* as a source for filling out and making explicit the original reasoning of *Proslogion* II and III. Accordingly, the third question to be considered is: how does the third or alternative interpretation explain the differences between the reasoning of *Proslogion* II and III and the reasoning of *Reply* I, the reasoning of *Reply* V, and the reasoning of *Reply* IX?

The answer to this question is not complicated. Once the reasoning of *Proslogion* II and III has been filled out and made explicit, the differences between that reasoning and the reasoning of *Reply* I, the reasoning of *Reply* V, and the reasoning of *Reply* IX are the differences between the original reasoning and emphasis on various steps in the series of deductions of that original reasoning. Once the reasoning of *Proslogion* II and III has been filled out and made explicit, it consists of a series of deductions which follow from a set of premises which contain the assumption that the being than-which-a-greater-cannot-be-thought does not exist, the assumption that the being than-which-a-greater-cannot-be-thought can be thought to exist, and a set of propositions which, according to Anselm, are implied by these assumptions. Accordingly, the reasoning of *Reply* I, the reasoning of *Reply* V, and the reasoning of *Reply* IX all represent emphasis on different and various steps in the series of deductions of the reasoning in *Proslogion* II and III, and, hence, they all also represent emphasis on different premises of that reasoning depending upon which premise is most prominently involved in the particular deduction.

Anselm's existential reasoning, whether it be the original reasoning or a discussion of that original reasoning, can be generally characterized as the procedure of showing that some proposition about the existence of the being than-which-a-greater-cannot-be-thought follows, given the assumption that the being does not exist and the assumption that the being can be thought to exist.

The Function of Reply I

When we turn to *Reply* I we see that its primary function is to answer the objection that even if the being than-which-a-greater-cannot-be-thought exists in the mind, it does not follow that it exists in reality. Anselm regards this objection as the primary challenge to be answered in *Reply* I, and he takes it not as a challenge to any of his original premises but as the challenge that his conclusion does not follow from his original premises. In order to answer this objection, then, Anselm must show not that his conclusion follows from some set of premises or other, but that his conclusion is deducible from his original premises when what is implicit in that original set of premises is made explicit. In fact, this is precisely what Anselm proceeds to do in the reasoning of *Reply* I, and there is nothing in his procedure which would suggest that he regards himself as providing any new premises that were not already implicit in the reasoning of *Proslogion* II and III. Anselm proceeds by arguing that if the being than-which-a-greater-cannot-be-thought can be thought to exist in reality, then given the assumption that the being does not exist, his conclusion does in fact follow; that is, Anselm proceeds by arguing that his conclusion is in fact deducible from his original premises and it is interesting to notice that his reasoning in *Reply* I has three distinct parts.

In the first part Anselm argues that (c) is deducible from his premises, in the second part he argues that (e) is deducible from his premises, and in the third part he argues that (d) is deducible from his premises; that is, in the reasoning of *Reply* I Anselm argues that his conclusion (c)-(d)-(e) is deducible from his original premises. But why does Anselm argue in *Reply* I that (d) and (e) are deducible from his premises? The challenge which Anselm is answering is the challenge that (c) does not follow from his premises. Does Anselm simply throw (d) and (e) in for good measure? The answer is obviously that he does not.

Anselm argues in *Reply* I that (c), (d), and (e) are all deducible from his premises because his existential conclusion is (c)-(d)-(e). The distinct assertions (c), (d), and (e) are all based on the same logical footing. Any challenge that (c) does not follow from Anselm's premises is also a challenge that (d) and (e) do not follow because (c), (d), and (e) are all deducible from the same set of premises. The assertion (c) is only part of Anselm's existential conclusion (c)-(d)-(e) about the being than-which-a-greater-cannot-be-thought; and while the deduction of (c), the deduction of (d), and the deduction of (e) all represent distinct steps in Anselm's series of existential deductions, it is a series of existential deductions from one set of premises.

Accordingly, the differences among the three distinct parts of the reasoning of *Reply* I represent emphasis on different steps in the series of deductions in the reasoning of *Proslogion* II and III, and they represent emphasis on different premises of the reasoning of *Proslogion* II and III depending upon which premise is most prominently involved in the particular deduction. The first part of the reasoning of *Reply* I represents both an emphasis on that step in the series of deductions whereby (c) is deducd from (F1) through (F8) and an emphasis on the premise which is most prominently involved in the deduction of (c) from (F1) through (F8), the second part of the reasoning of *Reply* I represents both an emphasis on that step in the series of deductions whereby (e) is deduced from (F1) through (F8) and an emphasis on the premise which is most prominently involved in the deduction of (e) from (F1) through (F8), and the third part of the reasoning of *Reply* I represents both an emphasis on that step in the series of deductions whereby (d) is deduced from (F1) through (F8) and an emphasis on the premise which is most prominently involved in the deduction of (d) from (F1) through (F8).

The First Part of Reply I: The Deduction of (c)

In the first part of the reasoning of *Reply* I, Anselm argues

> For 'that-than-which-a-greater-cannot-be-thought' cannot be thought save as being without a beginning. But whatever can be thought as existing and does not actually exist can be thought as having a beginning of its existence. Consequently, 'that-than-which-a-greater-cannot-be-thought' cannot be thought as existing and yet not actually exist.[13]

Since Np asserts that the being than-which-a-greater-cannot-be-thought cannot be thought to have a beginning and an end, and this is to assert that the being than-which-a-greater-cannot-be-thought cannot be thought save as being without a beginning, the first sentence of this passage can be symbolically represented by the formula Np.

Furthermore, since CKlNcp asserts that if the being than-which-a-greater-cannot-be-thought can be thought to exist in reality and it does not exist in reality, then it can be thought to have a beginning and an end, and since CKlNcp is equivalent to the substitution instance of the second sentence of this passage when that substitution is made with respect to "the being than-which-a-greater-cannot-be-thought," the second sentence of this passage can be symbolically represented by the formula CKlNcp. Finally, since the third sentence, the conclusion of this passage, asserts that if the being than-which-a-greater-cannot-be-thought can be thought to exist, then it does actually exist, the third sentence of this passage can be symbolically represented by the formula Clc. Accordingly, the entire passage can be represented in the following way:

(D32)   Np
(D40)   CKlNcp
        Consequently, Clc.

Now, Anselm's primary purpose in this passage is not to present a new argument or a variation or a version of some previous argument, rather Anselm's primary purpose in this passage is to answer Gaunilo's objection by arguing that (c) is deducible from (F1) through (F8) because (c) is deducible from the first two sentences of this passage. Since the second sentence of this passage asserts CKlNcp, the claim that (c) is deducible from the first two sentences of this

---

[13] *Ibid.*, pp. 169-171.

passage is equivalent to the claim that (c) follows from both the assumption that the being than-which-a-greater-cannot-be-thought can be thought to exist and the assumption that the being than-which-a-greater-cannot-be-thought does not exist, and the claim that (c) is deducible from the first two sentences of this passage represents the following deduction:

(D41) NKlNc   (from (D40) and (D32) by *Modus Tollens*)
(D42) ANlc   (from (D41) by De Morgan's Theorem)
(D43) Clc   (from (D42) by Implication)

Since Anselm assumes (l), that the being than-which-a-greater-cannot-be-thought can be thought to exist in reality, then

(D44) c

follows from (D43) and this assumption by *Modus Ponens*. Accordingly, Anselm is arguing that since (c) is deducible from the first two sentences of this passage, it follows that (c) is deducible from (F1) through (F8) because the first two sentences of this passage are deducible from (F1) through (F8). The claim that the first sentence of this passage is deducible from (F1) through (F8) represents the deduction:

(D28) CKqpj   (from (D6) by Commutation)
(D29) CqCpj   (from (D28) by Exportation)
(D30) q   (from (D5) and (D7) by *Modus Ponens*)
(D31) Cpj   (from (D29) and (D30) by *Modus Ponens*)
(D32) Np   (from (D31) and (D8) by *Modus Tollens*)

and the claim that the second sentence of this passage is deducible from (F1) through (F8) represents the deduction:

(D33) CNcm   (from (D2) and (D3) by Hypothetical Syllogism)
(D34) CNcp   (from (D33) and (D4) by Hypothetical Syllogism)
(D35) ACNcpNl   (from (D34) by Addition)
(D36) AAcpNl   (from (D35) by Implication)
(D37) ANlAcp   (from (D36) by Commutation)
(D38) AANlcp   (from (D37) by Association)
(D39) CNANlcp   (from (D38) by Implication)
(D40) CKlNcp   (from (D39) by De Morgan's Theorem)

Accordingly, in its secondary function this passage does not represent the introduction of any new concepts which are not already implicit in the original reasoning of *Proslogion* II and III and which cannot be made explicit in the reasoning of *Proslogion* II and III by appealing to principles which Anselm enunciates in other portions of the *Reply*, nor does this passage represent the introduction of principles which are independent of Anselm's axioms (F2) and (F3) about the relationship of reality to thought. Rather, this passage represents what can be deduced from (F1) through (F8) in order to deduce the third sentence, the conclusion, of this passage.

This passage represents intermediate steps in the deduction of (c) from (F1) through (F8). In its secondary function this passage represents emphasis on that step in the series of deductions whereby (c) is deduced in the reasoning of *Proslogion* II and III, and since CKlNcp is deduced primarily from (F2), (F3), and (F4), this passage represents emphasis on (F2), (F3), and (F4) as the premises which are most prominently involved in the deduction of (c) from (F1) through (F8).

The Second Part of Reply I: The Deduction of (e)

In the second part of the reasoning of *Reply* I Anselm argues

> But, whatever can be thought as existing and does not actually exist, could, if it were to exist, possibly not exist either actually or in the mind. For this reason, if it can merely be thought, 'that-than-which-a-greater-cannot-be-thought' *cannot not* exist.[14] (Italics mine.)

Again, Anselm assumes (l), that the being than-which-a-greater-cannot-be-thought can be thought to exist in reality, but in this passage he concludes his reasoning with (e), that the being than-which-a-greater-cannot-be-thought cannot not exist. What should be noticed here is that this passage immediately follows the first part of the reasoning of *Reply* I where Anselm has just finished establishing that (c) is in fact deducible in the reasoning of *Proslogion* II and III, that is, where Anselm has just established that it follows from his reasoning that the being than-which-a-greater-cannot-be-thought exists in reality. But the reasoning in the second part of *Reply* I is independent of the fact that (c) is in fact deducible from (F1) through (F8); that is, the deduction of (e) does not depend on the deduction of (c).

Anselm does *not* argue here that since the being than-which-a-greater-cannot-be-thought does exist in reality, it cannot not exist, rather Anselm argues that from the assumption that it does not exist,

---

[14] *Ibid.*, p. 171.

it follows that it cannot not exist. This, as we have already seen, is the procedure which is characteristic of Anselm's reasoning, and it is the same procedure which he employed in the reasoning of the first part of *Reply* I where he argues that from the assumption that the being than-which-a-greater-cannot-be-thought does not exist it can be shown that it follows that this being does exist in reality. In short, Anselm makes it quite plain that (c) and (e) both follow from the same considerations though the deduction of (e) represents a step distinct from the deduction of (c) and though the deduction of (e) and the deduction of (c) are mutually independent insofar as one can be deduced from (F1) through (F8) without the necessity of deducing the other as a step in the deduction of the first.

In the second part of the reasoning of *Reply* I Anselm points out that it follows that the being than-which-a-greater-cannot-be-thought cannot not exist because if it does not exist then it can not exist. Furthermore, Anselm claims here that this is the case even if this being were to exist; that is, Anselm hints here at what he makes explicit in the next part, namely, that there is more than one condition under which the assumption could be truthfully made that the being than-which-a-greater-cannot-be-thought does not exist. He hints here that even if this being were to exist under certain conditions, then the assumption that it does not exist could truthfully be made, and it would follow that this being can not exist.

So, what Anselm is pointing out here is that if the assumption can be made that this being does not exist, then it can not exist. Now, Anselm is arguing, if it can not exist then it can be thought not to exist, and if it can be thought not to exist, then it can be thought to have a beginning and an end. However, if it can be thought to have a beginning and an end and it can be thought not to have a beginning or an end, then it can be thought to be greater. But since it can be thought not to have a beginning or an end, it follows that if it can not exist, then it can be thought to be greater because if it can not exist, it can be thought to have a beginning and an end; and if it can be thought to have a beginning and an end, it can be thought to be greater. Hence, since it cannot be thought to be greater, it follows that the being than-which-a-greater-cannot-be-thought cannot not exist.

Anselm's primary purpose in this passage is to answer Gaunilo's objections by arguing that (e) is in fact deducible from (F1) through (F8). Accordingly, in its secondary function this passage represents emphasis on that step in Anselm's series of deductions whereby (e) is deduced in the reasoning of *Proslogion* II and III, and since the first sentence of this passage contains (F2) as part of its assertion, this passage represents emphasis on (F2) as the premise which is most prominently involved in the deduction of (e) from (F1) through (F8).

The Third Part of Reply I: The Deduction of (d)

In the third part of the reasoning of *Reply* I, after an elaborate and detailed discussion about the relationship of reality to thought, Anselm argues:

> Thus it is that whatever does not exist as a whole at a certain place and time can be thought not to exist, even if it does actually exist. But 'that-than-which-a-greater-cannot-be-thought' cannot be thought not to exist if it does actually exist; otherwise, if it exists it is not that-than-which-a-greater-cannot-be-thought, which is absurd. In no way, then, does this being not exist as a whole in any particular place or at any particular time; but it exists as a whole at every time and in every place.[15]

In the first two parts of the reasoning of *Reply* I, Anselm argues that some proposition about the existence of the being than-which-a-greater-cannot-be-thought does in fact follow from both the assumption that this being does not exist and from the assumption that it can be thought to exist; that is, Anselm argues that (c) and (e) are in fact deducible from (F1) through (F8). Similarly, Anselm argues in this passage that (d) is in fact deducible from (F1) through (F8); that is, Anselm argues that the proposition that the being than-which-a-greater-cannot-be-thought cannot be thought not to exist does in fact follow from both the assumption that this being does not exist and from the assumption that it can be thought to exist.

The difference between this passage and the first two parts of the reasoning of *Reply* I is that in this passage Anselm implicitly points out that there is a connection between the proposition that the being-than-which-a-greater-cannot-be-thought cannot be thought not to exist and the proposition that the being than-which-a-greater-cannot-be-thought cannot not exist, namely, that (d) is deducible if and only if (e) is deducible; and Anselm explicitly points out that there is a second condition under which the assumption could be truthfully made that the being than-which-a-greater-cannot-be-thought does

---

[15] *Ibid.*, p. 173.

not exist. Obviously that assumption could be truthfully made if this being does not in fact exist, but Anselm is claiming that the assumption could also be truthfully made if this being does in fact exist under certain conditions.

If the being than-which-a-greater-cannot-be-thought does not exist as a whole at every time and in every place, that is, if it can not exist because it fails to exist at some time or in some place or because it fails to exist in some part at some time or in some place, then it is true to say for some part of this being or for some place or for some time that it does not exist, even if it does exist in part or in some place or at some time. But if it does not exist in some part or at some time or in some place, then just as in the case when it does not exist at all, it can be thought not to exist. In short, what Anselm is saying is that if the assumption can be made that the being than-which-a-greater-cannot-be-thought does not exist, no matter under what conditions that assumption can be made, then this being can be thought not to exist.

As we have already seen, Anselm states explicitly in *Reply* III that if the being than-which-a-greater-cannot-be-thought can be thought not to exist, then it can be thought to have a beginning and an end. So, what Anselm is arguing in this passage is that if this being does not exist, then it can be thought not to exist (CNcm) and if it can be thought not to exist, then it can be thought to have a beginning and an end. However, if it can be thought to have a beginning and an end and it can be thought not to have a beginning or an end, then it can be thought to be greater. But since it can be thought not to have a beginning or an end and it cannot be thought to be greater, it follows then that it cannot be thought to have a beginning and an end. Hence, since it cannot be thought to have a beginning and an end, it follows that it cannot be thought not to exist.

Accordingly, what Anselm is arguing here is that from the assumption that the being than-which-a-greater-cannot-be-thought does not exist and the assumption that this being can be thought to exist, it follows that it cannot be thought not to exist. Furthermore, Anselm points out, since it cannot be thought not to exist, it follows that it exists as a whole at every time and in every place; that is, it follows that it cannot not exist because if it can not exist, it can be thought not to exist, and if it does not exist in some part or at some time or in some place, then it can not exist. What Anselm is pointing out here is that (d) and (e) both follow from the same considerations, that is, that (d) is deducible if and only if (e) is deducible.

Anselm's primary purpose in this passage is to answer Gaunilo's objection by arguing that (d) is deducible from (F1) through (F8) and by arguing that (e) is deducible from (F1) through (F8) if (d) is deducible from (F1) through (F8). Accordingly, in its secondary function this passage does not represent the introduction of any new premises which are not already implicit in the reasoning of *Proslogion* II and III, rather in its secondary function this passage represents emphasis on that step in Anselm's series of deductions whereby (d) is deduced in the reasoning of *Proslogion* II and III and whereby (e) can be subsequently deduced as well, and since the substitution instance CNcm of the first sentence of this passage follows from (F2) and (F3), this passage also represents emphasis on (F2) and (F3) as the premises which are most prominently involved in the deduction of (d) from (F1) through (F8) when (e) is to be subsequently deduced as well.

The Function of Reply V

When we turn to *Reply* V, we see that its primary function is to answer Gaunilo's general objection that Anselm's conclusion does not follow from the reasoning of *Proslogion* II and III. In his arguments Gaunilo's fundamental mode of criticism is to object, for various reasons, that Anselm's existential claims are not deducible for the being which Anselm identifies, but in his arguments Gaunilo uses the formula "that which is greater than everything" to describe the being which Anselm has identified as the being for which these existential claims are deducible. In order to answer this objection, then, Anselm must show not that his conclusion follows from some set of premises or other, rather Anselm must both point out that Gaunilo's objections are founded on a mistake, indeed, a very serious and all pervasive mistake, and show that his conclusion is in fact deducible from his original premises when what is implicit in that set of premises is made explicit.

In fact, this is precisely what Anselm proceeds to do in the reasoning of *Reply* V, and there is nothing in his procedure which would suggest that he regards himself as introducing any new principles or premises which were not already implicit in the reasoning of *Proslogion* II and III.

Anselm proceeds by first pointing out that Gaunilo's objections are founded on a mistake:

> For 'that which is greater than everything' and 'that-than-which-a-greater-cannot-be-thought' are not equivalent for the purpose of proving the real existence of the thing spoken of.[16]

and second by arguing that while the existential claims (c), (d), and (e) are not provable for that which is greater than everything, his conclusion does in fact follow from the assumption that the being than-which-a-greater-cannot-be-thought does not exist. In short, Anselm answers this objection, in part, by arguing that his conclusion is in fact deducible from his original premises and, furthermore, it is interesting to note that in *Reply* V Anselm states explicitly that the conclusion which follows from his reasoning is the conclusion (c)-(d)-(e).

Anselm makes it quite plain in *Reply* V that while the deduction of (c), the deduction of (d), and the deduction of (e) all represent separate and distinct steps in his series of deductions, (c), (d), and (e) are all deducible from the same set of premises; that is, they all follow from the assumption that the being than-which-a-greater-cannot-be-thought does not exist, the assumption that this being can be thought to exist, and a set of propositions which, according to Anselm, are implied by these assumptions. Accordingly, the reasoning of *Reply* V represents emphasis on the fact that (c), (d), and (e) are all steps in the series of deductions in the reasoning of *Proslogion* II and III, and it also represents emphasis on those premises of the reasoning of *Proslogion* II and III which are most prominently involved in the deduction of (c), (d), and (e) from (F1) through (F8).

In the reasoning of *Reply* V, after pointing out that the being which Gaunilo identifies is not equivalent to the being which he identifies, Anselm argues:

> Thus, if anyone should say that 'that-than-which-a-greater-cannot-be-thought' is not something that actually exists, or that it can possibly not exist, or even can be thought of as not existing, he can easily be refuted. For what does not exist can possibly not exist, and what can not exist can be thought of as not existing. However, whatever can be thought of as not existing, if it actually exists, is not that-than-which-a-greater-cannot-be-thought. But if it does not exist, indeed even if it should

---

[16] *Ibid.*, p. 179.

exist, it would not be that-than-which-a-greater-cannot-be-thought. But it cannot be asserted that 'that-than-which-a-greater-cannot-be-thought' is not, if it exists, that-than-which-a-greater-cannot-be-thought, or that, if it should exist, it would not be that-than-which-a-greater-cannot-be-thought. It is evident, then, that it neither does not exist, nor can not exist, or be thought of as not existing.[17]

According to Charlesworth, this passage is "yet another variation of the *Proslogion* argument." Charlesworth interprets this passage by saying:

> In this version 'that than which nothing greater can be thought' is defined as that which cannot be thought of as not existing. Now, 'what does not exist can possibly not exist, and what can not exist can be thought of as not existing.' Therefore, 'that than which nothing greater can be thought' must actually exist. Indeed, St. Anselm concludes, 'it neither does not exist, nor can not exist, or be thought of as not existing.'[18]

Now, Charlesworth's interpretation of this passage from *Reply* V is just as bewildering for what it implies as it is bewildering for what it states explicitly. It is obvious from the first and sixth sentences of this passage from *Reply* V both that Anselm distinguishes (c), (d), and (e) as separate and different assertions and that Anselm regards (c), (d), and (e) as having the same logical status in his reasoning. But Charlesworth explicitly states that Anselm, in this passage from *Reply* V, defines "the being than-which-a-greater-cannot-be-thought" as that which cannot be thought of as not existing; that is, according to Charlesworth, Anselm treats (d) as a definition. However, since (c), (d), and (e) all have the same logical status in Anselm's reasoning, if (d) is a definition, then Charlesworth's interpretation implies that Anselm defines into existence the being than-which-a-greater-cannot-be-thought because (c) and (e) would also be definitions as well. Surely, then, Anselm need not establish (c) in the reasoning of *Reply* V as Charlesworth represents him as doing, if "the being than-which-a-greater-cannot-be-thought" is defined as existing.

To be sure, this criticism of Charlesworth is only an *ad hominem* argument, but even so it shows either that Anselm ought not to have treated (c), (d), and (e) as definitions or that Charlesworth is mistaken in representing Anselm as having done so. Now while it is obvious that Anselm is claiming in this passage that (c) follows from both the

---

[17] *Ibid.*, pp. 179-181.
[18] *Ibid.*, pp. 95-96.

substitution instance (F2) and (F3) of the second sentence of this passage and assertion (d) by *Modus Tollens*, it is equally obvious that Charlesworth is mistaken in representing Anselm as treating (d) as a definition. Not only is it obvious from the first and sixth sentences of this passage that Anselm regards (c), (d), and (e) as having the same logical status, it is also obvious from the first sentence of this passage that Anselm regards (c), (d), and (e) not as premises in his reasoning but as conclusions deducible from his premises. In the first sentence of this passage Anselm explicitly states that if anyone should deny (c), (d) or (e) then that person can be refuted, and in the subsequent sentences of this passage Anselm shows how such a person could be refuted by showing how it is that (c), (d), and (e) are deducible from his premises.

Anselm's primary purpose in this passage is not to present a new argument or a variation or a version of some previous argument, rather Anselm's primary purpose in this passage is to answer Gaunilo's objections by arguing that (c), (d), and (e) are in fact deducible from (F1) through (F8) because "what does not exist can possibly not exist, and what can not exist can be thought of as not existing." What Anselm is arguing in these subsequent sentences is that (c), (d), and (e) are in fact all deducible from the assumption that the being than-which-a-greater-cannot-be-thought does not exist because that assumption implies that this being can not exist and this in turn implies that it can be thought not to exist, and this in turn indirectly implies that it can be thought to be greater. This reasoning occurs in this passage in two stages.

The Two Stages of Reply V:
The Deduction of (d) and the Deduction of (c) and (e)

In the third sentence of this passage Anselm is arguing that if a being is thought of, then if that being can be thought of as not existing then either that being is not the being than-which-a-greater-cannot-be-thought or if that being is the being than-which-a-greater-cannot-be-thought then that being cannot be thought not to exist because if that being can be thought of as not existing, then that being can be thought to have a beginning and an end and if that being can be thought to have a beginning and an end and that being can be thought not to have a beginning or an end, then that being can be thought to be greater. Now, since any being can be thought to be greater except the being than-which-a-greater-cannot-be-thought, either that being which is thought of is not the being than-which-a-greater-cannot-be-thought because that being *can* be thought to be greater, or if that being which is thought of is the being than-which-a-greater-cannot-be-thought, then that being which is thought of cannot be thought not to exist because that being *cannot* be thought to be greater. Accordingly, the first stage of Anselm's reasoning occurs in the third sentence of this passage, and in this stage of the reasoning Anselm shows that (d) is deducible from the denial of (d).

The second stage of Anselm's reasoning occurs in the fourth sentence of this passage, and in this stage Anselm shows that (c) and (e) are both deducible from the denial of (c) because the denial of (c) implies the denial of (e) and the denial of (e) implies the denial of (d). In the fourth sentence of this passage Anselm is arguing that since the claim that the being than-which-a-greater-cannot-be-thought does not exist implies that it can be thought not to exist (because if it does not exist then it can not exist and if it can not exist then it can be thought not to exist) and since the claim that it can be thought not to exist implies that it can be thought to be greater, it follows both that it cannot not exist and that it does exist because it cannot be thought to be greater.

In short, the second sentence of this passage represents emphasis on the set of premises (F2) and (F3) in Anselm's reasoning of *Proslogion* II and III; the third sentence represents both emphasis on the set of premises (F4) through (F6) in Anselm's reasoning of *Proslogion* II and III, and emphasis on the deduction of (d) from (F4) through (F6); the second and third sentences of this passage taken together represent emphasis on the connection between the set of premises (F2) and (F3) and the set of premises (F4) through (F6); and the fourth sentence of this passage represents emphasis on the deduction of (c) and (e) from (F2), (F3), and the deduction of (d) when the second and third sentences of this passage are taken together.

Accordingly, in its secondary function this passage does not represent the introduction of any new premises which are not already implicit in the original reasoning of *Proslogion* II and III, rather, in its secondary function this passage represents emphasis on the fact that the deduction of (c), the deduction of (d), and the deduction of (e) are all steps in the series of deductions in the reasoning of *Proslogion* II and III, and this passage also represents both emphasis on premises (F4) through (F6) as the premises most prominently involved in the deduction of (d) from (F1) through (F8) and emphasis on the premises (F2) and (F3) as the premises most prominently involved in the deduction of (c) and (e) from (F1) through (F8).

The Function of Reply IX

When we turn to *Reply* IX, we see that its primary function is to answer the objection that Anselm has not proved the real existence of the being than-which-a-greater-cannot-be-thought because his argument rests on the assumption that the being than-which-a-greater-cannot-be-thought can be thought of and understood when in fact the being than-which-a-greater-cannot-be-thought cannot be thought of nor understood. In order to answer this objection, then, Anselm must show not that he can prove the real existence of the being than-which-a-greater-cannot-be-thought from some premises or other, rather Anselm must instead show two things. Anselm must show that his assumption is true that the being than-which-a-greater-cannot-be-thought can be thought of and understood, and he must show that the real existence of the being than-which-a-greater-cannot-be-thought is deducible from his premises which rest upon that assumption; that is, Anselm must also show that either (c) or (e) is deducible from (F1) through (F8).

In fact, this is precisely what Anselm proceeds to do in the reasoning of *Reply* IX, and there is nothing in his procedure which would suggest that he regards himself as introducing any new principles or premises which are not already implicit in the reasoning of *Proslogion* II and III. Anselm proceeds by establishing three points. First, Anselm argues that from the denial of the existence of the being than-which-a-greater-cannot-be-thought, it follows that the term "the being than-which-a-greater-cannot-be-thought" is understood and thought of even if the object designated by that term cannot be thought of nor understood. This term is understood and thought of because whoever makes the denial thinks of and understands the denial and that denial cannot be thought of nor understood apart from its elements. Now, one of the elements of that denial is the term "the being than-which-a-greater-cannot-be-thought," so, Anselm reasons, whoever denies the existence of the being than-which-a-greater-cannot-be-thought thinks of and understands "the being than-which-a-greater-cannot-be-thought."

But Anselm is not satisfied with showing only that one can think of and understand "the being than-which-a-greater-cannot-be-thought." Since the being than-which-a-greater-cannot-be-thought is uniquely the being which cannot not exist, Anselm also sees that in order to answer Gaunilo's objection fully, it is necessary to establish two other points. Accordingly, Anselm points out that in the same way that one can think of and understand "the being than-which-a-greater-cannot-be-thought," one can also think of and understand the being which cannot not exist, and Anselm shows that the real existence of the being than-which-a-greater-cannot-be-thought (that it cannot not exist) is deducible from the assumption that it does not exist. In short, Anselm answers this objection by arguing that "the being than-which-a-greater-cannot-be-thought" can be thought of and understood, that the being which cannot not exist can be thought of and understood, and that the real existence of the being than-which-a-greater-cannot-be-thought is deducible from the denial of its existence. Accordingly, Anselm answers this objection in part by arguing that (e) is in fact deducible from his original premises when what is implicit in that set of original premises is made explicit, and the reasoning of *Reply* IX in part represents both emphasis on that step in the series of deductions whereby (e) is deduced in the reasoning of *Proslogion* II and III and emphasis on those premises of the reasoning of *Proslogion* II and III which are the premises most prominently involved in the deduction of (e) from (F1) through (F8).

The Reasoning of Reply IX: The Deduction of (e)

In the reasoning of *Reply* IX after showing both that "the being than-which-a-greater-cannot-be-thought" can be thought of and understood and that the being which cannot not exist can be thought of and understood and referring to the being which cannot not exist, Anselm argues:

> And one who thinks of this thinks of something greater than one who thinks of what can not exist. When, therefore, one thinks of that-than-which-a-greater-cannot-be-thought, if one thinks of what can not exist, one does not think of that-than-which-a-greater-cannot-be-thought. Now the same thing cannot at the same time be thought of and not thought of. For this reason he who thinks of that-than-which-a-greater-cannot-be-thought does not think of something that can not exist but something that cannot not exist.[19]

---

[19] *Ibid.*, p. 189.

In the first sentence of this passage Anselm points out two things. First, he points out that whenever someone thinks of a being, either he thinks of what cannot not exist or he thinks of what can not exist. The second thing Anselm points out is that what cannot not exist is greater than what can not exist, and hence, whoever thinks of what cannot not exist thinks of something greater than one who thinks of what can not exist. But the claim that what cannot not exist is greater than what can not exist does not represent the introduction of a new principle or premise independent of (F1) through (F8), rather the claim that what cannot not exist is greater than what can not exist is the consequence of (F1) through (F8), and hence, the claim that one who thinks of what cannot not exist thinks of something greater than one who thinks of what can not exist is not a new principle or premise but the consequence of (F1) through (F8). That this is the case should be apparent when we consider that Anselm assumes that the being than-which-a-greater-cannot-be-thought is greater than any other being which can be thought of and that for Anselm the being than-which-a-greater-cannot-be-thought is uniquely the being which cannot not exist. Now, if someone thinks of what cannot not exist, then it follows that he thinks of something greater than one who thinks of what can not exist because what cannot not exist is greater than what can not exist, but the claim that what cannot not exist is greater than what can not exist is itself true because what cannot not exist is the being than-which-a-greater-cannot-be-thought and the being than-which-a-greater-cannot-be-thought is greater than any other being which can be thought. For Anselm, then, the claim that what cannot not exist is greater than what can not exist cannot be used as a premise in his argument to establish that the being than-which-a-greater-cannot-be-thought cannot not exist because that claim assumes that the being than-which-a-greater-cannot-be-thought cannot not exist. That claim is not a premise for the conclusion (e), rather that claim is the consequence of the premises (F1) through (F8) from which (e) is deducible.

What Anselm is arguing in this passage is that the denial of the existence of the being than-which-a-greater-cannot-be-thought implies both that the being than-which-a-greater-cannot-be-thought cannot not exist and that what cannot not exist is greater than what can not exist, which is to say that the being than-which-a-greater-cannot-be-thought is greater than what can not exist. Anselm is arguing that whoever denies the existence of the being than-which-a-greater-cannot-be-thought either thinks of something which cannot not exist, or he thinks of something which can not exist, which is to say that if the denial is true, that is, if the being than-which-a-greater-cannot-be-thought does not exist, then the being than-which-a-greater-cannot-be-thought can not exist. Now, if he thinks of something which can not exist, then he thinks of something which can be thought not to exist, and if he thinks of something which can be thought not to exist, then he thinks of something which can be thought to have a beginning and an end; and, hence, he thinks of something which can be thought to be greater. But by assumption he is thinking of that than-which-a-greater-cannot-be-thought. Consequently, he is thinking of something which cannot without contradiction be thought to be greater, hence, he is thinking of something which cannot not exist. It follows, then, that the denial of the existence of the being than-which-a-greater-cannot-be-thought implies that the being than-which-a-greater-cannot-be-thought cannot not exist; it follows, that is, that (e) is in fact deducible from the assumption that the being than-which-a-greater-cannot-be-thought does not exist. Furthermore, since the being than-which-a-greater-cannot-be-thought cannot without contradiction be thought to be greater, whoever denies the existence of the being than-which-a-greater-cannot-be-thought is thinking of something greater than one who thinks of what can not exist, because what can not exist can without contradiction be thought to be greater.

In short, Anselm's primary purpose in this passage is to answer Gaunilo's objection in part by arguing that (e) is in fact deducible from (F1) through (F8). Accordingly, in its secondary function this passage does not represent the introduction of any new premises which are not already implicit in the reasoning of *Proslogion* II and III, rather, in its secondary function this passage represents both emphasis on that step in the series of deductions whereby (e) is deduced in the reasoning of *Proslogion* II and III and emphasis on (F2) and (F3) as the premises most prominently involved in the deduction of (e) from (F1) through (F8).

Anselm's Single Argument

In both the first and second chapters of this discussion, it was pointed out that Anselm claims to have provided in the *Proslogion* a single argument with which it can be proved whatever must be believed about the Divine Being, but it is manifest that the existential reasoning of *Proslogion* II and III is not, at least by itself, sufficient to prove any more than certain existential claims about the being than-which-a-greater-cannot-be-thought. The reasoning which has so far been identified is not by itself sufficient to prove that the being than-which-a-greater-cannot-be-thought bears the properties traditionally attributed to God.

Accordingly, the fourth question to be considered is: is it possible to identify in the *Proslogion* a single argument with which it can be proved whatever must be believed about the Divine Being? The answer to this question depends upon what is to count as a "single" argument. If by claiming to have provided a single argument, Anselm meant one set of premises from which both the existential claims and the theistic claims are deducible, then it is clear that a single argument cannot be identified because it is clear that no theistic claims are deducible from either (P1) through (P6) or (F1) through (F8).

But, if by a single argument Anselm meant a single argument form, then it is possible to identify in the *Proslogion* a single argument with which it can be proved whatever must be believed about the Divine Being. If in (P2) through (P6) we substitute for the word "exist" a word designating some theistic attribute, then it is possible to deduce from (P2) through (P6) the claim that the being than-which-a-greater-cannot-be-thought bears that attribute. For example, if in (P2) through (P6) we substitute the word "omnipotent" for the word "exist" then the result is a substitution instance of Anselm's single argument form from which it can be deduced that the being than-which-a-greater-cannot-be-thought is omnipotent.

Accordingly, if we leave blank the predicate places of (P2) through (P6) which are occupied by the word "exist," then that form of (P2) through (P6) represents Anselm's single argument. From that argument form it can be deduced that whatever must be believed about the Divine Being does in fact obtain for the being than-which-a-greater-cannot-be-thought. That this is in fact what Anselm meant is indicated in *Proslogion* V. In *Proslogion* V Anselm indicates that all of the theistic properties can, in a single sequence of deductions, be shown to obtain for the being than-which-a-greater-cannot-be-thought by completing the blank argument form with the predicate "whatever it is better to be than not to be," then, once it has been shown that (c), (d), and (e) all obtain for the being than-which-a-greater-cannot-be-thought, it can be deduced that the being than-which-a-greater-cannot-be-thought is whatever it is better to be than not to be. It remains, then, only to show both what properties there are which describe whatever it is better to be than not to be and that these properties can be consistently attributed to the being than-which-a-greater-cannot-be-thought. These last two tasks Anselm attempts to achieve in the remaining chapters of the *Proslogion*.

An Evaluation of Anselm's Reasoning

Now that Anselm's existential reasoning has been identified and the third or alternative interpretation explicated, there remains one task to be completed in order to fulfill the prescribed program of this discussion. There remains the task of evaluating Anselm's existential reasoning as it is identified by the third or alternative interpretation. It has already been pointed out that Anselm's existential reasoning is formally valid, so unless that reasoning is unsound, we must accept Anselm's conclusion (c)-(d)-(e) as established and true. But if Anselm's existential reasoning is unsound, then it must be because at least one of his premises is false and, unless it is logically false, a premise may be false for either one of two reasons. Either a premise is factually false, that is, it contradicts some empirical fact, or it is false by virtue of the fact that it is the result of some specifiable informal fallacy. In the first case an argument can be shown to be unsound by appealing to the relevant fact which falsifies the premise. In the second case an argument can be shown to be unsound by specifying the fallacious assumption upon which the premise rests. In theory, then, it is simple enough to know what needs to be done in order to demonstrate that an argument is unsound, but in practice it is not always so easy to show the falsity of a suspect premise because it is not always easy to do what must be done in order to show that a premise is false. That a premise is false and showing it to be false are two entirely different things. Quite often it is not possible to provide a refutation of an argument beyond showing that there is some very good reason for regarding one of its premises as false or at least as highly questionable. In some cases the best way to begin to show that one of the premises of an argument is questionable is to simply indicate by an analogical argument *that* there is a difficulty with the original argument and try to ascertain from a comparison of the two arguments where the difficulty lies. This, it seems, is the best procedure to adopt in evaluating Anselm's existential reasoning of *Proslogion* II and III.

If we change a few of the sentential elements of (F1) through (F8), the result is the following analogical argument to Anselm's existential reasoning:

(A1) If the being than-which-a-greater-cannot-be-thought does not exist in the mind alone, then it does exist in reality.

(A2) If the being than-which-a-greater-cannot-be-thought does exist in reality, then it can exist in reality.

(A3) If the being than-which-a-greater-cannot-be-thought can exist in reality, then it can be thought to exist in reality.

(A4) If the being than-which-a-greater-cannot-be-thought can be thought to exist in reality, then it can be thought not to have a beginning or an end.

(A5) If the being than-which-a-greater-cannot-be-thought can be thought not to exist in reality, then it can be thought to have a beginning and an end.

(A6) If the being than-which-a-greater-cannot-be-thought can be thought to have a beginning and an end and the being than-which-a-greater-cannot-be-thought can be thought not to have a beginning or an end, then the being than-which-a-greater-cannot-be-thought can be thought to be greater.

(A7) The being than-which-a-greater-cannot-be-thought can be thought not to exist in reality.

(A8) It is false that the being than-which-a-greater-cannot-be-thought can be thought to be greater.

Now, from (A1) through (A8) it can be deduced that:

(Ac) The being than-which-a-greater-cannot-be-thought does *not* exist in reality,

(Ad) The being than-which-a-greater-cannot-be-thought *cannot* be thought to exist,

and

(Ae) The being than-which-a-greater-cannot-be-thought *cannot* exist.

Depending upon whether we accept (F1) through (F8) or (A1) through (A8), we can justify either one of two contradictory sets of existential claims about the being than-which-a-greater-cannot-be-thought. The significance of this fact in evaluating Anselm's existential reasoning lies in the relationship between the A-reasoning and the F-reasoning. When we compare the two sets of premises, we see that Anselm is committed to (A8), (A6), (A5), and (A4) since these premises are identical respectively to (F8), (F6), (F4), and (F5). Furthermore, since (F2) is true on the basis of the modal principle that what is actual is possible and since (A2) is true on the basis of the same principle, then Anselm is also committed to (A2). The relationship between (F3) and (A3) is not quite so clear because it is not at all clear what is being asserted in the consequent of these conditional statements when it is claimed that something can be thought to exist or not to exist. But it would seem that the truth of (F3) depends, at least in part, on the principle that what is possible can be thought, and if Anselm accepts that principle, then surely he is also committed to (A3).

The relationship between (F1) and (A1) is also not very clear because if there are ways of existing in addition to existing in the mind and existing in reality, then there might be grounds for accepting (F1) as true which do not commit Anselm to accepting (A1) as true. However, this possible exception makes little difference since neither (F1) nor (A1) is required for the deduction of the conclusion from its respective set of premises. So far, then, while the F-reasoning is not identical to the A-reasoning, in accepting the F-reasoning Anselm is committed to accepting the A-reasoning, if accepting (F7) commits Anselm to accepting (A7).

What we need to know is whether or not accepting (F7) commits Anselm to accepting (A7) when (F7) and (A7) are considered independently of either the F-reasoning or the A-reasoning. However, it would seem that this is not very easily determined because it is not at all clear what is being asserted when it is claimed that something can be thought to exist or not to exist. The difficulty which arises can be made explicit if in (F7) and (A7) we replace the term "can" with the term "possible." When this is done (F7) is written:

(F7-1) It is possible that the being than-which-a-greater-cannot-be-thought is thought to exist in reality;

and (A7) is written:

(A7-1) It is possible that the being than-which-a-greater-cannot-be-thought is thought not to exist in reality.

Now, we have two compound statements each containing a sentential element which is itself a complete statement. Each of these compound statements asserts that some state of affairs is possible which is described by its sentential element. Accordingly, in order to understand what is being asserted as possible by these modal compound statements, it is necessary to understand what is being asserted in the sentential elements,

>   (F7-2) The being than-which-a-greater-cannot-be-thought is thought to exist in reality,

and

>   (A7-2) The being than-which-a-greater-cannot-be-thought is thought not to exist in reality.

The problem, then, of determining whether or not the acceptance of (F7) commits Anselm to accepting (A7) is the problem of determining what is being asserted when it is claimed that (F7-2) obtains and what is being asserted when it is claimed that (A7-2) obtains, and it is not at all clear what is being asserted in these two latter statements.

Unfortunately, Anselm gives us no help on this point. Anselm provides us with no indication of what is asserted by claiming either (F7-2) or (A7-2) and, hence, he gives us no indication of whether or not accepting (F7) commits him to accepting (A7). What is clear, though, is that if accepting (F7) commits Anselm to accepting (A7), then Anselm is committed to accepting both the conclusion (c)-(d)-(e) and the conclusion (Ac)-(Ad)-(Ae) and, hence, the conjunction (c)-(Ac), the conjunction (d)-(A7), and the conjunction (Ad)-(F7). But since the conjunctions (c)-(Ac), (d)-(A7), and (Ad)-(F7) are all clearly self-contradictory, accepting both (F7) and (A7) commits Anselm to a set of self-contradictory statements. What this shows is that Anselm's position is self-contradictory, if accepting (F7) commits him to accepting (A7). On the other hand, if accepting (F7) does *not* commit Anselm to accepting (A7) then whether Anselm accepts (c)-(d)-(e) or whether he accepts (Ac)-(Ad)-(Ae) depends simply upon whether he assumes (F7) or (A7). What this shows is that if accepting (F7) does not commit Anselm to accepting (A7), then Anselm must provide a justification for assuming (F7) rather than (A7). If no such justification is possible, then it is possible to justify a set of existential claims which are contradictory to Anselm's set of existential claims simply by assuming (A7) instead of (F7).

In short, the analogical argument shows either that Anselm's position is self-contradictory or that Anselm must justify his assumption (F7). As things now stand, either existential reasoning about the being than-which-a-greater-cannot-be-thought is self-contradictory, or any existential claims can be established about the being than-which-a-greater-cannot-be-thought by simply judiciously selecting the appropriate assumptions.

CONCLUSION

The prescribed program for this discussion has now been completed. The reasoning in and the relationship between *Proslogion* II and *Proslogion* III has now been identified and evaluated. The errors made by the proponents of the traditional interpretation and the errors made by the proponents of the new interpretation suggest a plausible third or alternative interpretation of *Proslogion* II and *Proslogion* III when those errors are examined in the light of what Anselm had to say both in the *Proslogion* and in the *Reply*. Anselm's purpose in *Proslogion* II and *Proslogion* III was not to establish the existence of God. Instead, these two Chapters represent one step in a larger program to establish whatever must be believed about the Divine Being, to establish that the being than-which-a-greater-cannot-be-thought exists and that the being than-which-a-greater-cannot-be-thought bears all the properties traditionally attributed to God.

Proslogion II and *Proslogion* III represent Anselm's effort to establish the existence and certain claims about the existence of the being than-which-a-greater-cannot-be-thought. But *Proslogion* II and *Proslogion* III have to be taken together in order to establish Anselm's existential claims. Neither *Proslogion* II nor *Proslogion* III contains a logically complete and independent argument. When these two Chapters are taken together they form the basis for a series of deductions which establish that the being than-which-a-greater-cannot-be-thought exists, that it cannot be thought not to exist, and that it cannot not exist. For Anselm, the form of this reasoning represents a single argument such that when certain of its predicate places are filled in by terms designating certain properties traditionally attributed to God, it can be deduced that the being than-which-a-greater-cannot-be-thought bears those properties. *Proslogion* V and the subsequent Chapters of the *Proslogion* represent Anselm's effort to establish these theistic claims and to establish the claim that the theistic attributes can be consistently predicated of the being than-which-a-greater-cannot-be-thought. When the existential claims, the theistic claims, and the consistency claim have all been established, then Anselm's program of demonstrating that God exists has been completed.

But if there is any meaning to the claim that the being than-which-a-greater-cannot-be-thought can be thought to exist in reality, then there is some similar meaning to the claim that the being than-which-a-greater-cannot-be-thought can be thought not to exist in reality. So, if instead of assuming that this being can be thought to exist in reality, it is assumed that this being can be thought not to exist in reality, then Anselm's argument form can be filled out in such a way that it forms the basis for a series of deductions which establish that the being than-which-a-greater-cannot-be-thought does not exist, that it cannot be thought to exist, and that it cannot exist. The result is either that Anselm's position is self-contradictory or else any existential claim can be established about the being than-which-a-greater-cannot-be-thought. Which of these alternatives obtains depends upon the relationship between the assumption that the being can be thought to exist in reality and the assumption that the being can be thought not to exist in reality. If the first of these assumptions commits Anselm to accepting the second, then Anselm's position is self-contradictory. If the first assumption does not commit Anselm to accepting the second, then some justification must be provided for accepting the first assumption and rejecting the second, or else on the basis of Anselm's own argument form, it is possible to establish that the being than-which-a-greater-cannot-be-thought does not exist.

BIBLIOGRAPHY

BOOKS

Anselm. *Saint Anselm: Basic Writings*. Translated by S. W. Dean with an introduction by Charles Hartshorne. La Salle, Illinois: Open Court, 1962.

Anselm. *St. Anselm's Proslogion with a Reply on Behalf of the Fool by Gaunilo and the Author's Reply to Gaunilo*. Translated with an introduction and philosophical commentary by M. J. Charlesworth. Oxford: The Clarendon Press, 1965.

Aquinas, St. Thomas. *Summa Contra Gentiles*. Translated by A. C. Pegis. Image Books. Garden City, New York: Doubleday & Company, Inc., 1955.

Barth, Karl. *Anselm: Fides Quaerens Intellectum*. Translated by I. W. Robertson. Richmond, Virginia: John Knox Press, 1958.

Descartes, René. *Philosophical Works of Descartes*. Vols. I and II. Translated by E. S. Haldane and G. R. T. Ross. New York: Dover Publications, Inc., 1955.

Hartshorne, Charles. *Anselm's Discovery*. La Salle, Illinois: Open Court, 1965.

Hartshorne, Charles. *The Logic of Perfection and Other Essays in Neoclassical Metaphysics*. La Salle, Illinois: Open Court Publishing Company, 1962.

Hartshorne, Charles. *Man's Vision of God*. Archon Books. Hamden, Connecticut, 1964.

Henry, D. P. *The Logic of Saint Anselm*. London: Oxford University Press, 1967.

Herrlin, Olle. *The Ontological Proof in Thomistic and Kantian Interpretation*. Uppsala: Lundequistska Bokhendeln, Uppsala University Arsskrift, No. 9, 1950.

Hick, John, ed. *The Existence of God*. New York: Macmillan Company, 1964.

Hick, John, and McGill, A. C., eds. *The Many-Faced Argument*. New York: Macmillan Company, 1967.

Kant, Immanuel. *Critique of Pure Reason*. Translated by N.K. Smith. London: Macmillan & Company, Ltd., 1958.

Leibnitz, G. W. *Discourse on Metaphysics and Correspondence with Arnauld*. La Salle, Illinois: Open Court Publishing Company, 1924.

Leibnitz, G. W. *New Essays Concerning Human Understanding*. Translated by A. G. Langley. La Salle: Open Court Publishing Company, 1949.

Leibnitz, G. W. *Philosophical Papers and Letters*. Translated by Leroy E. Loemker. Chicago: The University of Chicago Press, 1956.

McIntyre, John. *St. Anselm and His Critics*. Edinburgh: Oliver and Boyd, 1954.

Nakhnikian, George. *An Introduction to Philosophy*. New York: Alfred A. Knopf, 1967.

Plantinga, Alvin. *God and Other Minds*. Ithaca, New York: Cornell University Press, 1967.

Plantinga, Alvin, ed. *The Ontological Argument from St. Anselm to Contemporary Philosophers*. Anchor Books. Garden City, New York: Doubleday and Company, Inc., 1965.

Southern, R. W. *Saint Anselm and His Biographer*. London: Cambridge University Press, 1963.

PERIODICALS

Abraham, W. E. "Is the Concept of Necessary Existence Self-Contradictory?" *Inquiry*, 5 (1962), 143-157.

Alston, William P. "The Ontological Argument Revisited," *Philosophical Review*, 69 (1960), 452-474.

Armour, Leslie. "The Ontological Argument and the Concepts of Completeness and Selection," *Review of Metaphysics*, 14 (1961), 280-291.
Ballard, E. G. "On Kant's Refutation of Metaphysics," *New Scholasticism*, 32 (1958), 235-252.
Balz, A. G. "Concerning the Ontological Argument," *Review of Metaphysics*, 7 (1953-54), 207-224.
Baumer, William H. "Ontological Arguments Still Fail," *Monist*, 50 (January, 1966), 130-144.
Berg, Jan. "An Examination of the Ontological Proof," *Theoria*, 27-28 (1961-62), 99-106.
Bourke, Vernon J. "Invalid Proofs for God's Existence," *Proceedings of the American Catholic Philosophical Association*, 28 (1954), 36-49.
Discussion by:
    O'Neil, Charles L. "Some Comments on Dr. Bourke's Paper," *Proceedings of the American Catholic Philosophical Association*, 28 (1954), 50-54.
Broad, C. D. "Arguments for the Existence of God," *Journal of Theological Studies*, 40 (1939), 16-30, 156-167.
Broham, E. G. "Ontological Argument," *London Quarterly Review*, 157 (October, 1932), 522-529.
Buchanan, Scott. "Ontological Argument Redivivus," *Journal of Philosophy*, 21, No. 19 (1924), 505-507.
Carnes, R. D. "Descartes and the Ontological Argument," *Philosophy and Phenomenological Research*, 24 (1963-64), 502-511.
Charlesworth, M. J. "Linguistic Analysis and Language about God," *International Philosophical Quarterly*, 1 (1961), 137-167.
Cook, A. A. "The Ontological Argument and the Existence of God," *Proceedings of the Aristotelian Society*, 18 (1918), 363-384.
Crawford, Patricia. "Existence, Predication and Anselm," *Monist*, 50 (January, 1966), 109-124.
Davies, A. E. "Problem of Truth and Existence as Treated by Anselm," *Proceedings of the Aristotelian Society*, 20 (1919-1920), 167-190.
Dryer, D. P. "The Concept of Existence in Kant," *Monist*, 50 (January, 1966), 17-33.
Dwyer, Peter J. "Proving God," *Philosophical Studies*, 14 (Dublin, 1965), 7-29.
Earle, William A. "The Ontological Argument in Spinoza," *Philosophy and Phenomenological Research*, 11 (1950-51), 549-554.
Ebersole, F. B. "Whether Existence is a Predicate," *Journal of Philosophy*, 60, No. 18 (1963), 509-523.
Engel, S. M. "Kant's 'Refutation' of the Ontological Argument," *Philosophy and Phenomenological Research*, 24 (1963), 20-35.
Findlay, J. N. "Can God's Existence be Disproved?" *Mind*, 56-57 (1947-48), 176-183.
Discussion by:
    Findlay, J. N. "God's Non-Existence: A Reply to Mr. Rainer and Mr. Hughes," *Mind*, 58 (1949), 352-354.
    Hughes, George E. "Has God's Existence been Disproved? A Reply to Prof. J. N. Findlay," *Mind*, 58 (1949), 67-74.
    Hutchings, P. A. "Necessary Being and Some Types of Tautology," *Philosophy*, 39 (1964), 1-17.
    Rainer, A. C. A. "Necessity and God: A Reply to Prof. Findlay," *Mind*, 58 (1949), 75-77.
Flimons, Simon. "Kant and the Proofs for the Existence of God," *American Catholic Quarterly Review*, 48, No. 189 (1923), 14-48.
Franklin, R. L. "Necessary Being," *Australasian Journal of Philosophy*, 35, No. 2 (1957), 97-110.

Gaspard, Jerome. "On the Existence of a Necessary Being," *Journal of Philosophy*, 30, No. 1 (1933), 5-14.
Grant, C. K. "The Ontological Disproof of the Devil," *Analysis*, 17, No. 2 (1956), 71-72.
  Discussion by:
    Richman, R. J. "Ontological Proof of the Devil," *Philosophical Studies* (Minn.), 9 (1958), 63-64.
    Richman, R. J. "The Devil and Dr. Waldman," *Philosophical Studies* (Minn.), 11 (1960), 78-80.
    Waldman, Theodore. "A Comment upon the Ontological Proof of the Devil," *Philosophical Studies* (Minn.), 10 (1959), 49-50.
Grave, S. A. "The Ontological Argument of St. Anselm," *Philosophy*, 27 (1952), 30-38.
Hardin, C. L. "An Empirical Refutation of the Ontological Argument," *Analysis*, 22, No. 1 (1961), 10-12.
  Discussion by:
    Hardin, C. L. "Cows and Unicorns: Two Replies to Mr. Resnick," *Analysis*, 23, No. 1 (1962), 13-14.
    Keyworth, R. "Cows and Unicorns: Two Replies to Mr. Resnick," *Analysis*, 23, No. 1 (1962), 15-16.
    Resnick, L. "A Logical Refutation of Mr. Hardin's Argument," *Analysis*, 22, No. 4 (1962), 90-91.
    Resnick, L. "Do Existent Unicorns Exist?" *Analysis*, 23, No. 6 (1963), 128-130.
Harris, W. T. "Faith and Knowledge: Kant's Refutation of the Ontological Proof of the Being of God," *Journal of Speculative Philosophy*, 15 (1881), 404-428.
Hartford, R. R. "Fides Quaerens Intellectum," *Hermathena*, 74 (November, 1949), 1-8.
Hartman, Robert S. "Prolegomena to a Meta-Anselmian Axiomatic," *Review of Metaphysics*, 14, No. 4 (1961), 637-675.
Hartshorne, Charles. "The Logic of the Ontological Argument," *Journal of Philosophy*, 58, No. 17 (August, 1961), 471-473.
Hartshorne, Charles. "Rationale of the Ontological Proof," *Theology Today*, 20, No. 2 (July, 1963), 278-283.
Hartshorne, Charles. "What Did Anselm Discover?" *Union Seminary Quarterly Review*, 17, No. 3 (March, 1962), 213-222.
Hartshorne, Charles. "What the Ontological Proof Does Not Do," *Review of Metaphysics*, 17, No. 4 (June, 1964), 608-609.
Hartshorne, Charles. "The Formal Validity and Real Significance of the Ontological Argument," *Philosophical Review*, 53, No. 3 (May, 1944), 225-245.
  Discussion by:
    Elton, William. "On Hartshorne's Formulation of the Ontological Argument: a Criticism," *Philosophical Review*, 54, No. 1 (January, 1945), 63.
    Elton, William. "Professor Hartshorne's Syllogism: Criticism," *Philosophical Review*, 54, No. 5 (September, 1945), 506.
    Hartshorne, Charles. "On Hartshorne's Formulation of the Ontological Argument: A Rejoinder," *Philosophical Review*, 54, No. 1 (January, 1945), 63-65.
    Hartshorne, Charles. "Professor Hartshorne's Syllogism: Rejoinder," *Philosophical Review*, 54, No. 5 (September, 1945), 506-508.
Henry, D. P. "The *Proslogion* Proofs," *Philosophical Quarterly*, 5 (1955), 147-151.
Hick, John. "God as Necessary Being," *Journal of Philosophy*, 57, Nos. 22 and 23 (1960), 725-733.
Hintikka, Jaakko. "Studies in the Logic of Existence and Necessity," *Monist*, 50 (January, 1966), 55-76.

Hochberg, Herbert. "St. Anselm's Ontological Argument and Russell's Theory of Descriptions," *New Scholasticism*, 33 (1959), 319-330.
Hoernle, R. F. A. "Notes on the Treatment of 'Existence' in Recent Philosophical Literature," *Proceedings of the Aristotelian Society*, 23 (1922-1923), 19-38.
Huggett, W. J. "The Nonexistence of Ontological Arguments," *Philosophical Review*, 71 (1962), 377-379.
Huggett, W. J. "The *'Proslogion'* Proof Re-examined," *Indian Journal of Philosophy*, 2, No. 6 (1960-1961), 193-202.
Johnson, J. P. "The Ontological Argument in Plato," *The Personalist*, 44 (1963), 24-34.
Johnson, Oliver A. "God and St. Anselm," *Journal of Religion*, 45, No. 4 (1965), 326-334.
Johnston, T. A. "A Note on Kant's Criticism of the Arguments for the Existence of God," *Australasian Journal of Psychology and Philosophy*, 21, No. 1 (1943), 10-16.
Kearney, L. F. "Proofs of the Existence of God from the Metaphysical or Ideal Order," *The American Catholic Quarterly Review*, 16, No. 63 (1891), 462-474.
King-Farlow, J. "Existence and Proving Gods," *Darshana, An International Quarterly*, 1 (1961), 46-58.
Kiteley, M. "Existence and the Ontological Argument," *Philosophy and Phenomenological Research*, 18 (1958), 533-534.
Kiteley, M. "Is Existence a Predicate?" *Mind*, 73 (1964), 364-373.
La Fleur, Lawrence J. "The R-Being," *Philosophy of Science*, 9 (1942), 37-39.
Leydon, W. Von. " 'Existence': A Humean Point in Aristotle's *Metaphysics,*" *Review of Metaphysics*, 13 (1959-60), 597-604.
McDonald, H. D. "Monopolar Theism and the Ontological Argument," *Harvard Theological Review*, 58 (1965), 387-416.
MacIver, A. M. "A Note on the Ontological Proof," *Analysis*, 8, No. 3 (1948), 48.
Malcolm, Norman. "Anselm's Ontological Arguments," *Philosophical Review*, 69 (1960), 41-62.
Discussion by:
    Abelson, Raziel. "Not Necessarily," *Philosophical Review*, 70 (1961), 67-84.
    Allen, R. E. "The Ontological Arguments," *Philosophical Review*, 70 (1961), 56-66.
    Baier, K. E. M. "Existence," *Proceedings of the Aristotelian Society*, 61 (1960-1961), 19-40.
    Baumer, W. H. "Anselm, Truth and Necessary Being," *Philosophy*, 37 (1962), 257-258.
    Brown, T. P. "Prof. Malcolm on 'Anselm's Ontological Arguments'," *Analysis*, 22, No. 1 (1961), 12-14.
    Coburn, Robert C. "Professor Malcolm on God," *Australasian Journal of Philosophy*, 41 (August, 1963), 143-162.
    Henle, Paul. "Uses of the Ontological Argument," *Philosophical Review*, 70 (1961), 102-109.
    Huggett, W. J. "The Nonexistence of Ontological Arguments," *Philosophical Review*, 71 (1962), 377-379.
    Matthews, G. B. "On Conceivability in Anselm and Malcolm," *Philosophical Review*, 70 (1961), 110-111.
    Penelhum, Terence. "On the Second Ontological Argument," *Philosophical Review*, 70 (1961), 85-92.
    Plantinga, Alvin. "A Valid Ontological Argument," *Philosophical Review*, 70, No. 1 (January, 1961), 93-101.
    Ruja, Harry. "The Ontological Argument and a 'Living Faith'," *The Personalist*, 44 (1963), 293-301.

Yolton, J. W. "Prof. Malcolm on St. Anselm, Belief and Existence," *Philosophy*, 36 (1961), 367-370.

Zabeeh, Farhang. "Ontological Argument and How and Why Some Speak of God," *Philosophy and Phenomenological Research*, 22 (1961), 206-215.

Mascall, E. L. "Faith and Reason: Anselm and Aquinas," *Journal of Theological Studies*, 14, New Series (1963), 67-90.

Matson, W. I. "Basson's Ontological Argument," *Review of Metaphysics*, 12 (1958-59), 316-320.

Matthews, G. B. "Aquinas on Saying that God Doesn't Exist," *Monist*, 47 (1962-63), 472-477.

Mecklin, John M. "The Revival of the Ontological Argument," *Journal of Philosophy*, 14, No. 5 (1917), 124-135.

Miller, P. J. W. "The Ontological Argument for God," *The Personalist*, 42 (1961), 337-351.

Miller, Robert G. "The Ontological Argument in St. Anselm and Descartes," *Modern Schoolman*, 32 (1954-55), 341-349.

Miller, Robert G. "The Ontological Argument in St. Anselm and Descartes (Cont.)," *Modern Schoolman*, 33 (1955-56), 31-38.

Nakhnikian, G., and Salmon, W. C. " 'Exists' as a Predicate," *Philosophical Review*, 66 (1957), 535-542.

Nicholl, Donald. "An Anselmian Soliloquy," *Downside Review*, 68, No. 212 (Spring, 1950), 172-181.

Ogden, Schubert. "Theology and Philosophy: A New Phase of the Discussion," *Journal of Religion*, 44, No. 1 (1964), 1-16.

Paullin, William T., Jr. "A Review of the Ontological Arguments," *American Journal of Theology*, 10, No. 1 (1906), 53-71.

Penelhum, Terence. "Divine Necessity," *Mind*, 69 (1960), 175-186.

Potter, Vincent G. "Karl Barth and the Ontological Argument," *Journal of Religion*, 45, No. 4 (1965), 309-325.

Prior, A. N. "Is Necessary Existence Possible?" *Philosophy and Phenomenological Research*, 15 (1954-55), 545-547.

Puccetti, Roland, "The Concept of God," *Philosophical Quarterly*, 14 (1964), 237-245.

Rescher, Nicholas. "The Ontological Proof Revisited," *Australasian Journal of Philosophy*, 37 (August, 1959), 138-148.
    Discussion by:
        Gunderson, K., and Routley, R. "Mr. Rescher's Reformulation of the Ontological Proof," *Australasian Journal of Philosophy*, 38 (December, 1960), 246-252.

Richardson, Cyril C. "The Strange Fascination of the Ontological Argument," *Union Seminary Quarterly Review*, 18 (November, 1962), 1-21.
    Discussion by:
        Brkic, Jovan. "Further Fascination of the Ontological Argument: Replies to Richardson," *Union Seminary Quarterly Review*, 18 (March, 1963), 246-249.
        Comstock, W. Richard. "Further Fascination of the Ontological Argument: Replies to Richardson," *Union Seminary Quarterly Review*, 18 (March, 1963), 250-255.
        Hartshorne, Charles. "Further Fascination of the Ontological Argument: Replies to Richardson," *Union Seminary Quarterly Review*, 18 (March, 1963), 244-245.

Ross, James F. "God and 'Logical Necessity'," *Philosophical Quarterly*, 11 (1961), 22-27.
    Discussion by:

Williams, C. J. F. "God and 'Logical Necessity'," *Philosophical Quarterly*, 11 (1961), 356-359.
Ruja, Harry. "The Definition of God and the Ontological Argument," *Australasian Journal of Philosophy*, 41 (August, 1963), 262-263.
Runyan, Mary Edith. "The Relationship between Ontological and Cosmological Arguments," *Journal of Religion*, 43, No. 1 (1963), 56-58.
Ryle, Gilbert. "Mr. Collingwood and the Ontological Argument," *Mind*, 44 (1935), 137-151.
  Discussion by:
    Harris, E. E. "Mr. Ryle and the Ontological Argument," *Mind*, 45 (1936), 474-480.
    Ryle, Gilbert. "Back to the Ontological Argument," *Mind*, 46 (1937), 53-57.
Rynin, David. "On Deriving Essence from Existence," *Inquiry*, 6, No. 2 (1963), 141-156.
Scott, Frederick. "Scotus, Malcolm, and Anselm," *Monist*, 49 (1965), 634-638.
Scott, G. E. "Quine, God, and Modality," *Monist*, 50 (January, 1966), 77-86.
Shaffer, Jerome. "Existence, Predication and the Ontological Argument," *Mind*, 71 (1962), 307-325.
Shedd, William G. T. "The Ontological Argument for the Divine Existence," *Presbyterian Review*, 5 (1884), 213-227.
Sheldon, W. H. "Necessary Truths and the Necessary Being," *Journal of Philosophy*, 26, No. 8 (1929), 197-209.
Sheldon, W. H. "Another Form of the Ontological Proof," *Philosophical Review*, 32 (1923), 355-372.
  Discussion by:
    Sheldon, W. H. "Statistical Law and the Ontological Proof," *Philosophical Review*, 33 (1924), 286-289.
    Smart, H. R. "Statistical Law and the Ontological Proof," *Philosophical Review*, 33 (1924), 73-82.
Smart, H. R. "Anselm's Ontological Argument: Rationalistic or Apologetic?" *Review of Metaphysics*, 3 (1949-50), 161-166.
Smith, Gerald. "Before You Start Talking about God," *Modern Schoolman*, 23 (1945), 24-43.
Smith, J. Macdonald. "How Do We Prove that God Exists?" *Downside Review*, 79, No. 256 (1961), 217-231.
Webb, C. C. J. "Anselm's Ontological Argument for the Existence of God," *Proceedings of the Aristotelian Society*, 3, No. 2 (1894-96), 25-42.
Wells, Norman J. "Existence: History and Problematic," *Monist*, 50 (January, 1966), 34-43.
Werner, Charles G. "The Ontological Argument for the Existence of God," *Personalist*, 46 (1965), 269-283.
Wild, John. "The Concept of Existence," *Monist*, 50 (January, 1966), 1-16.
Wolter, Allen B. "Duns Scotus and the Existence and Nature of God," *Proceedings of the American Catholic Philosophical Association*, 28 (1954), 94-121.
Wolz, Henry G. "The Empirical Basis of Anselm's Arguments," *Philosophical Review*, 60 (1951), 341-361.
Wolz, Henry G. "The Function of Faith in the Ontological Argument," *Proceedings of the American Catholic Philosophical Association*, 25 (1951), 151-163.
Woollen, C. J. "The Ontological Morass," *Homiletic and Pastoral Review*, 43 (1943), 893-900.
Zabeeh, Farhang. "On Necessary Existence," *Indian Journal of Philosophy*, 3 (1962), 227-233.